SECULOSITY

SECULOSITY

HOW CAREER, PARENTING,
TECHNOLOGY, FOOD,
POLITICS, AND ROMANCE
BECAME OUR NEW RELIGION
AND WHAT TO DO ABOUT IT

DAVID ZAHL

SECULOSITY
How Career, Parenting, Technology, Food, Politics, and Romance Became Our
New Religion and What to Do about It

Cover design: Laura Drew
Cover image: GoodStudio/Shutterstock.com

Print ISBN: 978-1-5064-4943-2
eBook ISBN: 978-1-5064-4944-9

The paper used in this publication meets the minimum requirements of American National Standard for Information Sciences — Permanence of Paper for
Printed Library Materials, ANSI Z329.48-1984.

Manufactured in the U.S.A.

For my special guys: Charlie, Cabell, and Tommy

Half the harm that is done in this world
Is due to people who want to feel important.
They don't mean to do harm—but the harm does not
  interest them.
Or they do not see it, or they justify it
Because they are absorbed in the endless struggle
To think well of themselves.

—T. S. Eliot

The most purely, proudly American genre of writing
  might be the to-do list.

—Parul Sehgal

CONTENTS

Introduction		xi
Chapter 1	The Seculosity of Busyness	1
Chapter 2	The Seculosity of Romance	17
Chapter 3	The Seculosity of Parenting	41
Chapter 4	The Seculosity of Technology	65
Chapter 5	The Seculosity of Work	87
Chapter 6	The Seculosity of Leisure	105
Chapter 7	The Seculosity of Food	121
Chapter 8	The Seculosity of Politics	135
Chapter 9	The Seculosity of Jesusland	161
Conclusion: What to "Do" about It		185
Acknowledgments		193
Endnotes		195

INTRODUCTION

'll give you *one* clue," Sherry said, baiting me to guess where she and her family were moving. "It's a place where no one's religious but everyone is super religious."

"That doesn't exactly narrow it down," I responded, trying to match her cynicism.

She smiled, but I knew she wasn't making the observation lightly. Sherry had grown up in the sort of strict religious household about which prestige dramas are made. The more you learned about her childhood, the more miraculous it became that she maintained any faith at all.

As a result, she could smell piety in the air like pizza. It was her superpower. There's nothing quite like the anxiety of the devout, she would tell me, or the kind of shame that's marshalled in defense of orthodoxy.

I remember asking her once why she wasn't angrier. It seemed to me that Sherry had every reason to hate religion and anyone associated with it. Her answer has stayed with me: she told me that one of the great wake-up calls of adulthood came when she realized that religiosity was not confined to churchgoers or those who checked the "belief" box in the latest Pew survey. In fact, for those who'd had a particularly heavy dose in their formative years, it was hard not to see religiosity—and its fallout—everywhere.

It wasn't the first time I had heard this. Tales of friends who'd left small towns for big cities in search of a more open-minded environment, only to discover that their new surroundings weren't as orthodoxy-free as they'd hoped, had become almost cliché. It sounds like a *Portlandia* sketch, but it is empirically true: the religious impulse is easier to rebrand than to extinguish.

This runs counter to popular perception. Bombarded with poll results about declining levels of church attendance and belief in God, we assume that more and more people are abandoning faith and making their own meaning. But what these polls actually tell us is more straightforward. They tell us that confidence in the religious narratives we've inherited has collapsed. What they fail to report is that the marketplace in replacement religion is *booming*. We may be sleeping in on Sunday mornings in greater numbers, but we've never been more pious. Religious observance hasn't faded apace "secularization" so much as migrated—and we've got the anxiety to prove it. We're seldom *not* in church.

That's a bold assertion to make, I know, and one that depends greatly on your definition of *religion*.[1] If you're going with the common conception—of robes and kneeling and the Man Upstairs, what we might call capital-R Religion—then, yes, people are bailing in unprecedented numbers.

Some say this has to do with science, some with capitalism, or moralism, or distraction, or indifference, or whatever. The roots of so-called secularization aren't that important, at least not for the purposes of this book. What's important is that it's happening and will in all likelihood continue to.

---

1. And *secular.*

The landscape shifts, however, if you opt for a more expansive view of religion. For instance, as sanctuaries in Europe have emptied, folkloric beliefs have thrived. A majority of Icelanders claim to believe in hidden creatures like elves and about a third of Austrians in lucky charms (not the cereal). Half of Sweden gives credence to mental telepathy. According to AppStore downloads, millennials in the United States are increasingly enamored of astrology.

Tempting as occult belief systems such as these may be, this book sets out to look at how the promise of salvation has fastened onto more everyday pursuits like work, exercise, and romance—and how it's making us anxious, lonely, and unhappy.

Perhaps a more helpful definition of religion comes from writer David Dark. He calls it "a controlling story" or "the question of how we dispose our energies, how we see fit to organize our own lives and, in many cases, the lives of others."

According to this definition, religion is not merely that which explains the inexplicable but the lens through which you sort the data of your days, rank your priorities, and focus your desires. We'll call this small-r religion. A person's *religion* is shorthand for the shape that lens takes—namely, the specific ways it refracts what we see and directs our longings. This can be a set of unconscious assumptions about the world, or it can be a perspective that's deliberately adopted, like an *-ism* of some kind. Most often, it's both.

While a solid starting point, I wonder if Dark's definition veers a tad too close to that dreaded term *worldview*. Because religion in real life is more than a filter or paradigm. It is what we lean on to tell us we're okay, that our lives matter, another name for all the ladders we spend our days climbing toward a dream of wholeness. It refers to our preferred guilt-management system. Our small-r religion is the *justifying* story of our life. Ritual and community and all the other stuff come second.

A conventional person of faith would likely insert something here about religion having to do with worship. They would have a point. But *worship* is such a tricky word. It carries a judgment that makes it awkward to use when most applicable. It can imply a certain servility or weak-mindedness. More than that, most talk of worship tends to frame it as a conscious pursuit, suggesting that life is simply a matter of finding the right thing to worship and doing so, rather than the continued frustration of venerating the wrong thing(s), despite knowing better. Furthermore, we fail to recognize that what we're actually worshipping when we obsess over food or money or politics is not the thing itself but how that thing makes us *feel*—if only for a moment.

Our religion is that which we rely on not just for meaning or hope but *enoughness*.

Enough's Enough?

Listen carefully and you'll hear that word *enough* everywhere, especially when it comes to the anxiety, loneliness, exhaustion, and division that plague our moment to such tragic proportions. You'll hear about people scrambling to be successful enough, happy enough, thin enough, wealthy enough, influential enough, desired enough, charitable enough, woke enough, *good* enough. We believe instinctively that, were we to reach some benchmark in our minds, then value, vindication, and love would be ours—that if we got enough, we would *be* enough.

But here's the wrinkle, one so well worn it hardly bears mentioning: no matter how close we get or how much we achieve, we never quite arrive at *enough*. (How much money is enough, Mr. Rockefeller? Just a little bit more.) Our lives attest that the threshold does not exist, at least not where fallible and finite human beings are concerned. Instead, "people are suffering and dying under the torture of the fantasy self they're failing to become."

This is not a secret. Pretty much every wisdom tradition lays it plain. Nevertheless, we spend our days chasing the mirage, often to the detriment of our well-being and that of our neighbors. What gives?

The answer has something to do with the research that moral psychologist Jonathan Haidt recounts in his book *The Righteous Mind*. He writes in the introduction that "an obsession with righteousness . . . is the normal human condition." The longing for some form of righteousness is not an aberration perpetuated by capital-R Religion but a foundation of what it means to be human. In other words, we cannot shake the specter of enoughness because it lives in our DNA. This obsession is invaluable when it comes to the formation of groups and survival of the species. But there are significant downsides.

Experience, not to mention the Bible, confirms the veracity of Haidt's claim. We want to feel good about ourselves, and so we edit our personalities to maximize the approval of others. Or we exaggerate hardships to make ourselves seem more heroic or others more villainous. The theological and psychological term for the energy we expend for the sake of feeling righteous is *self-justification*, and it cannot be overstated as a motivation in human affairs.

If you want to understand what makes someone tick, or why they're behaving the way they are, trace the righteousness in play, and things will likely become clear. Your colleague who can't stop working? Odds are, she equates busyness with worthiness. Your perpetually single friend who can't seem to find someone who measures up to his standards? It could be that he's looking to another person to "complete" him—to make him feel like he's *enough*.

What about you? Maybe the reason you can't stop scrolling through your social-media feed is because it confirms how right(eous) your opinions about others or yourself are. Or maybe, on some level you can barely admit to yourself, you believe that if your latest post on Facebook gets enough likes, you will finally like yourself.

Wherever you are most tired, look closely and you'll likely find self-justification at work, the drive to validate your existence—to assert your lovability—via adherence to some standard of enoughness, be it behavioral or conceptual, given or invented.

While *enoughness* may not be a direct synonym for *righteousness*, it's not far off. After all, *enough* only makes sense if there's some kind of line demarcating it from *not enough*. It implies a standard of some kind. Yet we avoid the word *righteousness* because it sounds too religious, too old-fashioned, too judgy, too close to *self-righteous*—and we know we don't like *that*. *Righteous* sounds ominously absolute and therefore authoritarian, as though it could impinge on the lives of those around us. *Enough*, on the other hand, has a more subjective and therefore less threatening connotation.

In practice, there's very little difference. Those dogged by a sense of *not-enoughness* know all too well that "I'll know *enough* when I see/feel it" isn't any lighter of a burden than "reach [X, Y, or Z] objective standard." Both are classic spiritual treadmills, and the former may even be more taxing due to its slipperiness. Whatever the case, the problem of self-justification is not a linguistic one.

The Deeper Pathos

A major problem for those of us with "righteous minds" comes when our conception of righteousness differs from that of our neighbors, or when we feel they are standing in the way of our attainment of it. Innocuous-seeming differences in perspective balloon overnight into showdowns over good versus evil. And nothing allows us to excuse ruthlessness easier than when we've painted our neighbor as an adversary to all that is true and holy.

I'm not just talking about digital mobs and their penchant for public shaming and heresy hunting. I'm talking about heartache and divorce and job loss and estranged children.

There's a deep irony at work here: enoughness is a universal human longing. The yearning for it binds us together across party, country, gender, race, and age. It provides the glue that holds our most altruistic movements together. Yet, the specific expression of this obsession in each person's life is often what alienates us from others. The tighter the in-group, the larger the out-group will be. Depending on the *content* of the righteousness in question, this drive can spark our most dehumanizing judgments of other people and inspire us, sometimes unconsciously, to conceive of the world in terms of us versus them.

Doubtless this is what theologian Reinhold Niebuhr meant when he observed that "there is no deeper pathos in the spiritual life of man than the cruelty of righteous people." He was referring to what Christians call Pharisaism—an overreliance on superficial indicators of righteousness that in practice bely their opposite (e.g., following the letter of the law to the degree that it contradicts the spirit). Jesus did not have an easy time with the Pharisees.

How sad that Christianity today has a reputation for self-righteousness that's more akin to Pharisaism than the gracious ethos of its founder. Too often that reputation is well deserved. What people don't always see is that the same oppressive spirit afflicts replacement religions, too. Self-righteousness tends to follow self-justification, regardless of backdrop.

Which is to say, Niebuhr's aphorism is well designed for our times. People who think they're good are usually pretty mean. They often feel good *about* being mean. As my friend Sherry never tires of reminding me in regard to her fundamentalist upbringing, a culture dominated by outward demonstrations of piety will become an increasingly merciless place, full not only of self-justification but self-consciousness and fear. It will be a place that crucifies rather than forgives.

That said, most of us don't need a modern-day Pharisee in the room before we start to feel bad about falling short. We have one in our heads already! An inner accountant who takes copious notes on our failures. How else do we account for the fact that the most accomplished people feel more, rather than less, pressure to succeed? Or that people who are better-looking perceive their blemishes so acutely?

The truth is that the higher we climb on the ladder of self-justification, the longer it gets—and the further apart the rungs grow. You might say that the cost of an ideal of righteousness is the reality of unrighteousness, pure and simple. Whether or not we have the resources to cope with that burden is a different question.

Why is it that we seem more fixated on righteousness, on enoughness, than any time in recent memory? At the risk of gross oversimplification, for centuries we relied on capital-R Religion to tell us that we're okay. Clergy revealed not only the shape of true righteousness but also how we might come to be associated with it. Church provided us a place to go with our guilt and shame. For more and more people in the modern world, that no longer feels like an advisable or available option.

Some, like Friedrich Nietzsche, predicted that we would find peace in the deconstruction and emerge into a new and gloriously liberated mode of human existence. Without a divine law to make us feel poorly about ourselves, words like *guilt* would lose their meaning. We would no longer need any lens to buffer us from the unsightly aspects of reality; we would have the courage to face things head-on. A glorious, post-religious age of human flourishing would dawn.

Alas, if our current cultural climate tells us anything, it's that the needs addressed by Religion—for hope, purpose, connection, justification, enoughness—haven't diminished as churches have become taprooms and theaters. The psychic energy involved hasn't evaporated. It can't. It has to go *somewhere*.

With altars off the table, fresh targets have cropped up all over the place, from the kitchen to the gym to the computer screen to the bedroom. Righteousness, you might say, is running amok and breeding mercilessness wherever it goes. Where once we chose between an array of different schools to attend, now there's the *one* that will ensure our future success—and the many that will squander it. Where once there was a sea of a nice people to date, now there's Mr./Ms. Right—and everyone else is a waste of our time.

It may be easy to shrug off such notions when we see them on the printed page, but it's a different story when our children are applying to college, or when we're deciding to ask for a promotion at work. These myths exercise enormous influence emotionally—some part of us simply can't help but believe them. Those Icelanders may be onto something after all.

What's more, it often seems that the further we retreat from a shared Religion, the more contenders emerge to harness our floundering religiosity. Philosopher Charles Taylor calls this "the nova effect," likening it to an explosion of religious pluralism.

If that's too highfalutin, think of the arcade game *Centipede*: cutting off the head of the centipede doesn't kill the beast but divides it into a bunch of extra-dangerous little children. The more fearsomely you slash, the more nefarious the multiplication. These new religions go by different names but function more or less the same, maintaining all the demand (and much of the ritual!) but none of the mercy of the capital-R variety. If we used to go to church once a week, we now go every hour. It's exhausting, to put it mildly.

I aim to survey a few of the more popular religions-that-aren't-called-religions out there today for a couple of reasons. First, I am convinced that this way of interpreting our pursuits is not only inherently interesting but has deep explanatory power vis-à-vis contemporary culture. Second, I believe that questioning our knee-jerk reactions against either religion *or* secularism by recognizing that these impulses are everywhere, that none of us are truly free of them, can only expand the shrinking common ground that's required to live together in a nonmiserable way.

In peeling back the veneer of fading Religion, I am confident that we'll find compassion for others who are just as enrapt to their righteous minds as we are. We may even find that we understand ourselves a bit better. Who knows, our tour might reveal to us a fresh and enlivening vision of twenty-first-century enoughness. You'll have to read to the end to find out.

Rhymes with Velocity

Most people don't like being told they're religious—and not just those who identify as atheists. The ever-increasing demographic of the "spiritual but not religious" suggests that *religion* is a dirty word across the board. What's more, there does seem to be a discernible difference between grounding your hope in something material and something spiritual. Blanketing both groups with such a loaded label could come off as patronizing.

Which is why I am proposing a fresh term: *seculosity*. I'm using it as a catchall for religiosity that's directed horizontally rather than vertically, at earthly rather than heavenly objects.

Perhaps *secular* warrants its own explanation, though. My most immediate association comes from the beloved sitcom *Arrested Development*, where the repressed wife of a pastor begs one of the godless protagonists to "take me to your *secular* world." What she meant, presumably, is an environment without the divine as its default, where the metaphysics are up for grabs (and people are having a bit more fun). *Secular*, in this sense, serves not as a synonym for *a-religious* or *materialistic*, as is often assumed today. It is simply a descriptor of any setting in which belief in God is not axiomatic.

Furthermore, many forms of seculosity are pursued alongside explicitly Religious forms of devotion. This means that no one, by virtue of how they self-identify (or spend their Sunday mornings), is exempt from our diagnosis. The most public Christian you know may be just as ensconced in various forms of seculosity as anyone else. It doesn't make their belief necessarily insincere. It's simply evidence that they are subject to the same conflicting temptations and fears as you are. Your author certainly is.

In fact, it's worth acknowledging this may sound suspiciously like a case of the man with the hammer thinking everything's a nail. I am someone, after all, who was once referred to as "that religious guy" in a pre-wedding reply-all fiasco among my wife's friends. Not a flattering description, but not off base either: the bulk of my professional life *has* been spent in the employ of Religious organizations and churches. At the same time, the bulk of my *personal* life—upbringing, education, friendships—has been spent as the only religious guy in the room, the one who, like it or not, has been called upon to translate in both directions for as long as I can remember.

While I may have an investment in the notion that religion—and religious faith—sits at the center of human experience, you don't have to harbor that same conviction to acknowledge that religion may possess valuable resources for understanding and negotiating our current crisis. At the very least, those resources should not be ignored. If runaway piety is truly part of what's poisoning our well-being today, then a familiarity with the way religions operate can only be a help. I cannot guarantee these pages are 100 percent vacant of confirmation bias (who could?!), but I *can* pledge that I have done my utmost to vacuum out the more overt rationalizations, taking care to reference predominantly non-Religious sources.

It should also be said, up front, that the waxing religiosity traced herein is by and large something I find lamentable, not vindicating. Seculosity inspires anxiety rather than comfort—both in myself and others—and that bums me out. What discourages me even more, however, is the pretense that we're not just as puritanically devout as we have ever been.

One last qualification: my chief trepidation in writing a book like this is that I would communicate a disdain for the phenomenon I am describing, that I'm somehow above it rather than a co-belligerent and co-beneficiary. Rest assured, there is nothing here I am not exploring from the inside.

The objects of our seculosity—food, romance, education, children, technology, and so on—aren't somehow bad. Quite the opposite—they are by and large great. It's only when we lean on these things for enoughness, when we co-opt them for our self-justification or make them into arbiters of salvation itself, that they turn toxic. My aim throughout, therefore, is to temper criticism with affection. Poking fun at our secular pieties, including my own, is part of disarming them.

That's where I'm placing my faith, anyway. I hope you'll take the leap with me.

By the way, the place Sherry was talking about? San Francisco.

CHAPTER 1

THE SECULOSITY
OF BUSYNESS

The picture shows cartoon villain Cruella de Vil, bloodshot eyes staring straight ahead, hands clutching the wheel of her infamous coupe, black-and-white hair waving wildly in the wind, oversized fur coat flapping behind. In a word: crazed. Over the image someone has typed:

> Me trying to excel in my career, maintain a social life, drink enough water, exercise, text everyone back, stay sane, survive and be happy.

Beneath the meme, a caption reads, "every day." It's followed by a string of comments, "Amen," "Yep," "Like lookin' in a mirror," and so on. People can relate, and not just the same old suspects. A quick survey of the peanut gallery's profiles and you can't help but notice the breadth of demographics represented, male and female, old and young, black and white. (Then again, it's Instagram, so who can say for sure?)

But this much is clear: it takes one of Disney's trippiest images to capture the white-knuckle pace of modern life. If only what we were chasing with such fanatical intensity was a van full of dalmatians.

You don't need a clever meme to deduce this. Just ask the next person you see how they're doing. The stock reply used to be "fine" or "well." Today, there's a very good chance they'll respond with "busy."

Reflexive and unoriginal as the answer may be, it is not dishonest. Take my friends Jen and Ted. They are currently balancing two full-time careers with raising three young children. Anyone who follows their family on social media knows that Ted is coaching T-ball this spring and Jen can hardly keep up with the demand that her side hustle—making bespoke placemats and selling them on Etsy—is generating. Less public would be the fact that Ted's father has recently been diagnosed with early onset Alzheimer's, and the papers on Jen's sister's divorce have yet to be signed.

So when I asked them the other day how they're doing and they responded with an emphatic "busy!" they weren't lying.

What bothered me about the interaction was not their answer so much as the way it reminded me of how I must sound when using that same word—which I do at least ten times a day. Some version of the following:

Q: Dave, what's the latest?

A: Oh, you know how it is, busy as a banshee. Wheels coming off the bus any day now! Definitely looking forward to things slowing down.

It sounds like I'm complaining about the super abundance of activity, when in truth I actually prefer it that way. Idleness makes me far more uncomfortable than busyness, a blank to-do list considerably more nerve-wracking than an overstuffed one. What would it mean about me if I didn't have enough commitments to fill my schedule? Nothing good, that's for sure.

I am hardly the first to note how ubiquitous busyness has become in our day-to-day. Or how transparently reassuring. To be busy is to be valuable, desired, justified. It signals importance and, therefore, enoughness. Busy is not just how we are but *who* we are—or who we'd like to be.

As with Jen and Ted, this does not mean we don't have a ton on our plates. We do. The demands on our time, and for our attention, only seem to increase with each passing year, growing ever more frenetic and unforgiving. Advertisers have begun to talk of the dawn of "the attention economy" for good reason. Some chalk the escalation up to a changing global economy, some to smart technology, some to post-Christian spiritual restlessness. Whatever the case, "busy" is no longer the sole purview of high-octane professionals and parents of toddlers. Everyone I know is busy, and hardly anyone frames it as a conscious choice. If anything, it feels like the only means of survival.

I used to wonder if busyness was primarily a matter of context. Surely if we moved away from the coast and into the country, if we simplified, we would be less harried, more present. Journalist Brigid Schulte put that theory to the test while doing research for her 2014 book, *Overwhelmed.* She traveled to North Dakota and convened a group of farmers to talk about their lives:

You'd think, wouldn't [the North Dakotans] enjoy their lives more, wouldn't they have more time for what's important?

But, sitting around that focus group table, every single person was stressed out of their minds. One woman said the only leisure time she'd had was when she was awaiting her mammogram in the doctor's office.

In other words, pathological busyness is not confined to the streets of Manhattan or the LA freeway. Even among what used to be called "the leisure class," busyness now serves as a barometer of personal enoughness and, therefore, justification. The more frantic the activity, the better. The implication, of course, is that if we're not over-occupied, we are inferior to those who are. Busyness has become a *virtue* in and of itself.

This is not a neutral phenomenon. Research on the issue paints a foreboding picture, health-wise. Unremitting busyness reliably predicts chronic stress, and therefore heart disease, sleeplessness, higher blood pressure, and shorter life spans, to say nothing of general fatigue.

But so what if I'm exhausted? At least I feel accomplished. Well, talk to any marriage counselor and they will tell you that worse than anger or guilt in marriage is weariness. That's when the relationship is really on the rocks, when you're too tired to fight, or no longer see the point of another attempt at rapprochement. The same can be true when it comes to your relationship with yourself.

As tired as it makes us, busyness remains attractive because it does double duty, allowing us to feel like we're advancing on the path of life while distracting us from other, less pleasant realities, like doubt and uncertainty and death. When we move rapid-fire from task to task we (theoretically) minimize the mental space available for painful feelings, at the same time accruing extra points in the enoughness column, whether they be material or emotional or both. So we stay busy to keep the rivers of affirmation and reward flowing in our direction. We are afraid they will stop if we're not generating the current.

No wonder so many of us wear our exhaustion as a badge of honor. Complaining of being "crazy busy" may be today's definitive #humblebrag.

Elsewhere in her book, Schulte consults University of North Dakota researcher Ann Burnett, who has spent a prodigious amount of time collecting and analyzing Americans' Christmas letters. Her findings are sadly predictable. Among the five decades worth of letters in her archive, those from recent years focus far less on giving thanks or forecasting the future and much more on how jam-packed the preceding months have been. She cites one particularly vivid example, in which a mother writes:

> I'm not sure whether writing a Christmas letter when I'm working at the speed of light is a good idea, but given the amount of time I have to devote to any single project, it's the only choice I have. We start every day at 4:45 AM, launch ourselves through the day at breakneck speed, only to land in a crumpled heap at 8:30 PM, wondering how we made it through the day.

Burnett characterizes such letters as marked by a "busier than thou" attitude, in which people unconsciously (or not) compete over who has more going on. The religious language ("thou") is no accident.

If the protagonists in Jane Austen novels gloried in their idleness—their distance from the harried lower echelons of society who have no choice *but* to work—a couple centuries later the opposite holds sway: "keeping up with the Joneses now means trying to out-schedule them." Busyness has become a status symbol, a.k.a. a public display of enoughness.

For an increasing amount of the population, then, to be alive in the twenty-first century is to wonder privately how much longer you can keep feeding the beast before you keel over.

The very phrase *feed the beast* could not be more apt. It conjures the image of a ravenously hungry creature whose appetite demands satiation, lest it carve out its pound of flesh. It brings to mind a prowling monster that can be momentarily appeased but never fully satisfied. A life of feeding the beast recasts our activities, and the rewards they bring, as momentary offerings on the anxious altar of Enough.

A little melodramatic, I know, but hopefully the description rings some bells. Because what we're talking about when we talk about chronic busyness is *performancism*, one of the hallmarks of all forms of seculosity.

Performance Almighty

Performancism is the assumption, usually unspoken, that there is no distinction between what we *do* and who we *are*. Your resumé isn't part of your identity; it *is* your identity. What makes you lovable, indeed what makes your life worth living, is your performance at X, Y, or Z. Performancism holds that if you are not doing enough, or doing enough well, you *are* not enough. At least, you are less than those who are "killing it."

Billy Mitchell makes for an entertaining case in point. You may remember him from the 2007 documentary *King of Kong*, which shone a spotlight on the colorful quest for the world's highest score at the Donkey Kong arcade game. As the film opens, Billy holds the record. He's something of a legend in the classic gaming community, and you can see why: a dramatic mullet and an American flag necktie tucked into his jeans give him the swagger of an eighties rock star.[2]

Billy wastes no time in explaining to the camera that "there's a level of difference between people, and it translates into some games." He tells us that "since I debuted on the scene in 1982, there hasn't been anyone . . . who's played even close." The filmmakers then survey a group of his fellow competitors. "When Billy Mitchell walks into an arcade, everything stops. There's electricity about him. Everyone wants to crowd around him," one gushes. Another comments, "If you could hack into the machine and program it to play itself, you couldn't even program it that well." The next goes so far as to say—with a straight face—that "everything about him is perfect." The segment concludes with Billy's father proudly proclaiming, "He's a winner. Billy Mitchell is a winner."

In the eyes of his peers, his family—and, let's face it, himself—Billy has become synonymous with his video-game performance. There's no difference between the initials in the high-scores ranking and the numbers sitting next to them. Unlike most of us, however, Billy *has* fulfilled all righteousness. He is worshipped for his accomplishment, and the veneration seems to suit him.

As the film goes on, we realize that the perch at the top of the ladder, even a ladder as quaint as the little ones that adorn a Donkey Kong screen, is not as magnificent as it looks. When a fellow competitor comes out of nowhere and threatens Billy's

---

2. WWF superstar is probably more accurate.

hegemony, the situation does not bring out the best in the defending champion or his henchmen. The ensuing hijinks and manipulations are the fruit of what happens when performance becomes synonymous with identity, and while hilarious, they're not pretty.[3]

Don't be deceived by the relatively low (read: absurd) stakes here. The same lesson applies in far more serious and less palatable situations: losing may hurt, but in a performancist paradigm so does winning—just in a different and more deceptive way. Apart from some momentary gratification, victory doesn't usher in contentment or peace so much as fear, paranoia, and the pressure to maintain. Feed the beast, or else.

Performancism turns life into a competition to be won (#winning) or a problem to be solved, as opposed to, say, a series of moments to be experienced or an adventure to relish. Performancism invests daily tasks with existential significance and turns even menial activities into measures of enoughness. The language of performancism is the language of scorekeeping, and just like the weight scale or the calendar, it knows no mercy. When supercharged by technology, the result can even be deadly.

The Kids Are Not Alright

Our devotion to the dogmas of performancism lies at the root of much of the skyrocketing anxiety, loneliness, and fatigue that saddle so many hearts and minds today.

---

3. I'm sure I wasn't the only one who cracked a smile when Billy was stripped of his records in 2017, after evidence emerged that he'd submitted bogus scores.

We see this devotion particularly, but not exclusively, in young people. To wit, the rash of "suicide clusters" in affluent areas of the United States (Palo Alto, CA; Northern Virginia; Western Chicago; Fairfield County, CT; etc.). These are places afflicted by high-school suicide rates four and five times the national average, high-achieving enclaves where the pressure to meet the highest possible standards of academic and athletic excellence has left those prone to self-harm even more isolated than adolescence already accomplishes on its own.[4]

By no means is the phenomenon limited to secondary schools, though. Elite colleges have long served as clusters unto themselves. The University of Pennsylvania made national headlines when the campus witnessed an astounding six student suicides in a thirteen-month stretch in 2013–14. In response, the administration formed a task force to study mental health on campus. Their final report cited something called "Penn Face," defined as "the practice of acting happy and self-assured even when sad or stressed." Penn Face, the authors surmised, derives from the "perception that one has to be perfect in every academic, cocurricular and social endeavor." *Effortlessly* perfect, that is; only the most casual mastery will get you to the top of the Ivy League scoreboard.

Spending excessive amounts of time in this mode "can manifest as demoralization, alienation or conditions like anxiety or depression." Expectation and isolation are a fatal combination.

After Penn released its report, the *New York Times* followed up with an article of its own in which they profiled an undergraduate

---

4. According to the cover story of the December 2015 issue of *The Atlantic Monthly*, 12 percent of Palo Alto high-school students surveyed in the 2013–14 school year reported having seriously contemplated suicide in the past twelve months.

named Kathryn DeWitt. She recalled how upset she had been upon learning that she had scored, uncharacteristically, in the sixties on a calculus exam. "I had a picture of my future, and as that future deteriorated, I stopped imagining another future," she confessed to journalist Julie Scelfo. Following the news of a beloved classmate's suicide around the same time, Ms. DeWitt contemplated taking a similar route.

That is a *lot* of power to ascribe to a single grade on a single exam. Then again, when we're gripping the wheel as tightly as Cruella, even the slightest nudge can steer us over the cliff. One incontrovertible failure may be all it takes to confirm whatever deeper doubts we harbor about ourselves, and in a world devoid of redemption—a state of mind exacerbated by depression—self-harm is merely the instantiation of the damnation already enacted upon us. Perhaps this explains, at least in part, why some people would rather end their lives than confess that they've lost their jobs or made a bad investment.

Make no mistake, any scheme where salvation is reserved for those with the most impeccable track records is a *religious* scheme.[5] It may be unconscious, but that only makes the dynamics involved more dangerous.

---

5. This is the precise understanding of religion parodied so brilliantly in the sitcom *The Good Place*, in which it is revealed that people accrue points during their time on Earth according to their deeds. Their sum total determines whether they go to "the good place" or "the bad place" when they die. For example, remaining loyal to the Cleveland Browns nets you +53.83 points, while overstating a personal connection to a tragedy that has nothing to do with you will ding you −41.84 points. It's telling that the performancism is both universally and immediately recognizable to audiences and its pitfalls so endlessly entertaining.

Paradise Will Not Be Pixelated

Virtually every discussion of on-campus suicide references the omnipresence of social media. You don't have to be familiar with Leon Festinger's "social comparison theory" from the 1950s to know that we instinctually determine a great deal of our worth based on how we stack up against others, no matter our stage or station in life. The thirtieth high-school reunion is seldom less onerous than the fifth one.

Smart phones have ushered in an era where such comparisons are both unceasing and meticulously curated. The competitive righteousness displayed on our little screens naturally accelerates, fostering increasingly stratospheric expectations of performance that all but mandate constant shortfall and the attendant anxiety. Thus, the sense of not-enoughness—via social condemnation— has become more pronounced as the demographics using the technology have exploded in breadth.[6]

A study published in 2018 in *International Journal of Information Management* established empirically what we all know experientially: the more time people spend on Facebook, the happier they perceive their friends to be and the sadder they feel as a consequence. The longer we spend on social media, the more that our screen starts to resemble the high-score rankings screen of Life (and not the Milton Bradley version).

---

6. The percentage of adults aged sixty-five and older who own smartphones more than doubled between 2013 and 2017, from 18 percent to 42 percent. Social-media use stats are not far behind. On the opposite end of the spectrum, according to a 2018 study, the average age of receiving one's first smartphone dropped from twelve to ten between 2012 and 2017.

Furthermore, insofar as social media operates as a vehicle of comparative judgment, it also operates as a vehicle of isolation, one that leaves us feeling more alone in our less-than-rosy reality than we might otherwise be, blind to the truth that our profile may be inspiring the same exact feelings in others.

Perhaps you remember the well-publicized story of Essena O'Neill, the Australian model who bailed on over half a million Instagram followers in late 2015. O'Neill had spent the preceding three years amassing an enormous following on the platform, enough to garner sponsorships to make her both wealthy and admired by legions of fans. Yet at the height of her influence she confessed, "16-year-old Essena would have been like 'WTF girl you have the dream life.' So why did I feel so lost, lonely and miserable?"

One day she reached her breaking point and decided to edit the captions on the pictures of herself that had received the most response. Next to what appeared to be a casual selfie she wrote,

> Please like this photo. I put on makeup, curled my hair, tight dress, big uncomfortable jewelry. . . . Took over 50 shots until I got one I thought you might like, then I edited this one selfie for ages on several apps—just so I could feel some social approval from you. THERE IS NOTHING REAL ABOUT THIS #celebrityconstruct

Mercifully, few of us reach Essena's level of exposure. Some of us may even experience social media as positive and helpful, but hardly anyone who uses these platforms will be unfamiliar with what she describes.

Of course, performancism predates the internet by a long shot. Arcade games too. No doubt plenty of Betty Draper-type mothers in the 1950s would have been able to relate to the Cruella de Vil meme. I know for a fact that first-century Palestinians understood the virtue of keeping up appearances at any cost.

No, presentation anxiety is not unique to postmillennial life. Nor is it a purely secular force. In fact, some of the most toxically performancist environments exist inside the church, where anxious people frantically try to outdo one another in the good-works department, whether those be acts of charity or acts of devotion or both—as if our spiritual resumé was the ticket to God's approval. While few would ever admit to such outright heresy, believers often can't help measuring themselves against their fellow congregants, dropping hints of how often they read their (heavily underlined) Bible, how much money they give, or how many shifts they pick up at the soup kitchen. In lieu of "Penn Face" you have "Sunday Face."

Faith that more often than not begins with an admission of losing and need morphs into a hectic competition for spiritual justification, in which we baptize our busyness with religious language. Soon, God has ceased to be a good shepherd and turned into the Taskmaster-in-the-Sky, or worse, another name for the persecutor within. The targets may be ostensibly more righteous, but the exhaustion and anxiety they produce are identical to their secular correlates. "I just couldn't keep it up anymore!" is the refrain I've heard from many a refugee from performancist churches.

More than that, the pressure to uphold a veneer of perfect holiness creates all manner of dysfunction and double lives. Just consult the seemingly endless parade of celebrity pastors who have "fallen from grace."[7]

---

7. A popular misnomer, as grace is something you fall *into*, not from—a tad nitpicky, but still.

If there's a difference today, it has to do with the vanishing of outlets where the pressure of perfection might be vented. It's easier to develop a sense of enoughness, for example, when your pool of peers is in the hundreds rather than the millions, when the primary venues of comparison close shop at 5:00 p.m. Similarly, it's a lot harder to recover from a youthful indiscretion when the internet has made the record of your adolescence permanent and searchable.

Capital-R Religion once provided a space to come clean and maybe even be absolved of shortcoming and guilt. Church wasn't busy. If anything, it was boring and full of silence, a respite from the noise of daily demand, a place to receive rather than achieve. The good ones at least.

A Bushel of Plums

Churches devoid of performancism may have largely vanished from the landscape, but the glimpses they offered, at their best, of an alternative way of approaching ourselves and the world still flit across our line of sight from time to time, thank God. When it happens, we don't forget.

In her memoir *Cherry*, Mary Karr recounts just such an instance. When she was fourteen years old, while her parents were out of the house, a miserable Mary tried to do herself in by swallowing a handful of pills. She was unsuccessful and wound up sick. When her mother and father returned home, they tenderly nursed her, without suspecting the suicide attempt. They attributed the vomiting to food poisoning.

After a while, her father asked her if there was any food she could stomach. All she thought she could eat would be a plum. But plums were out of season, and so she went to bed.

The next morning, her father came into her room with a bushel of plums, having driven through the night from Texas to Arkansas to get them for her. Mary remembers:

> But it's when you sink your teeth into the plum that you make a promise. The skin is still warm from riding in the sun in Daddy's truck, and the nectar runs down your chin.
>
> And you snap out of it. Or are snapped out of it. Never again will you lay a hand against yourself, not so long as there are plums to eat and somebody—anybody—who gives enough of a damn to haul them to you. . . . That's how you acquire the resolution for survival that the coming years are about to demand. You don't earn it. It's given.

In that blinding instant, the justifying story of Mary's life switched tracks, her performance revealed to be at best beside the point, at worst a liability, when it came to what really mattered. And what mattered was the magnitude of the uncoerced generosity, so towering and inconceivable in proportion to the not-enoughness that had clouded her vision.

Unlike Cruella, she hadn't even needed to get behind the wheel.

CHAPTER 2

THE SECULOSITY
OF ROMANCE

My decade of peak wedding attendance is just about behind me. And by that, I mean my thirties. Cousins, siblings, friends of mine from high school and college—and those of my wife's—they're pretty much all hitched at this point. My closet is filled with ties I'll never wear again.

The experience has been neither cheap nor boring. If fifteen years ago you had rattled off the list of settings I'd shuffle into for people's big days, I doubt I would've believed you: backyards, rooftops, vineyards, art galleries, restaurants, night clubs, closed-circuit TVs—oh, and churches.

Same goes for the ceremonies themselves. I've attended weddings officiated by a friend, a family member, a priest, a boss, some random justice of the peace, even a shaman. A good proportion followed an established religious script or liturgy, others were composed by the couple themselves, and a number have been collaborative with the audience. I've been on hand for a couple of disasters (fires, fainting, an absent groom) but the vast majority went smoothly.

There's clearly no one-size-fits-all when it comes to the day itself. Weddings I expected would be indulgent or awkward have turned out to be fun and touching and full of joy. Weddings I figured would be sweet and reverent have been stressful and full of tension.

But that doesn't mean there aren't a few ties that, well, bind. For instance, I have never been to a wedding where the couple hasn't been described as "perfect" for each other, or where the relationship in question hasn't been characterized as "right." And even those ceremonies where G-O-D gets some burn from up front, the real deity on hand almost always goes by the name Cupid. (Not that the two are mutually exclusive![8])

As should already be evident, it is virtually impossible not to sound gloomy when surfacing the seculosity of romance. Don't shoot the piano player, though: aim for cultural anthropologist Ernest Becker instead.

Back in 1973, in his just-as-upbeat-as-you'd-imagine book *The Denial of Death*, Becker prophesied the wedding industry's explosive growth when he introduced the idea of *apocalyptic romance*. To fill the void left by capital-R Religion, Becker claimed, we turn first and foremost to romance. "The love partner becomes the divine ideal within which to fulfill one's life. All spiritual and moral needs now become focused in one individual."

Becker foresaw what many of us experience every time we attend a wedding, that there is no more fertile ground for seculosity than romance and relationships. Let's run down the checklist:

---

8. Though one highly doubts that the apostle John had chocolate and roses in mind when he wrote that "God is love."

- Do we look to romantic love to tell us we're enough? Check.
- Do our relationships often house our primary guilt-management system? Check.
- Does romance provide a (theoretical) route to transcendence and salvation? Check, check.
- Do we ritualize it into oblivion? Hey now.

Eighth Grade Never Ends

If you're confused, just think back to middle school, when the performancism of relationships reaches an early peak. Middle schoolers make little-to-no distinction between who they are and who likes them (or *likes them*, likes them). In middle school, we believe with all our hearts that if we are liked by the right people, especially the right girl or boy, we will be enough. It's when we first spiritualize our social and romantic aspirations; our crush becomes the focus of every prayer. Each interaction with another person becomes an occasion for performance—a heavy burden for any thirteen-year-old. Or fifty-year-old, as the case may be.

More than affection, what we're looking for in eighth grade is approval, the validation not that we're loved so much as lov*able*. How cruel, then, that the defining sensation of middle school—self-consciousness—has a way of repelling the opposite sex, whereas self-confidence attracts. What sounds like a double bind makes a funny kind of sense: if we're looking to another person to accept us in order to feel good about ourselves, then our attention will be focused on how well or badly we are doing every time we're around them, and not on the other person themselves. We will be scanning their words and movements for clues about where we stand rather than listening to what they may actually be trying to communicate.

We grow taller and move on to other grades and schools, but that inner eighth-grader and his relational performancism never disappears entirely. Perhaps we become skilled enough at projecting our likability that we convince someone to stick around. After the initial wave of euphoria and relief subsides, if we still like them, we embark on the project of making them stay, which is much more arduous if you can't take your eyes off your personal scoreboard.

Literary critic Stanley Fish chalks up the dissolution of his first marriage to this sort of performancism. For him, social engagements felt more like tests he had to pass than times to enjoy other people's company. Parties were something to *get through*. "This way of interacting or, rather, not interacting does not augur well for intimate relationships," he later confessed. "If you characteristically withhold yourself, keep yourself in reserve, refuse to risk yourself, those you live with are not going to be getting from you what they need." He includes his children in the list of those who suffered from his fear of coming up short, socially.

You cannot get close to someone who is using you to prop up their enoughness. Sustaining love—the kind that won't vanish but flourish in the midst of vulnerability and setback—cannot find oxygen until performancism has run its course.

Which is a longwinded way of saying: you can't have a lasting relationship with an eighth-grader.

All Roads Lead to NYC (and All Roads in NYC Lead to Our Apartment)

It's not just *who* we relate to that can become our justifying story but *how* we relate to them.

A few years after getting married, my wife and I moved into an apartment on what is commonly considered the busiest block in New York City, 60th Street between 2nd and 3rd Avenue, a.k.a. the off-ramp to the Queensboro bridge, a.k.a. the main entrance point into Manhattan for commercial traffic as well as one of its prime shopping districts.

Night and day, eighteen-wheelers rolled past our window and taxis honked their horns. Gazillions of tourists flocked to Bloomingdale's next door. If all roads lead to New York City, then all roads in New York City led to our apartment. Sure, the rent was amazing and the apartment relatively spacious, but we were living in the middle of a highway.

Having lobbied for the move, I felt responsible. But instead of breaking the lease the moment we realized how bad the noise was, I spent the next six months not-so-subtly trying to convince my better half of the positives of our predicament. "I love having the subway on our corner," I would passive-aggressively tell her. "The restaurant downstairs sure has some good pizza."

Whenever she got discouraged about how absurdly unpeaceful our living situation was, instead of empathizing with her I would feel judged. Sensing criticism, my inner lawyer kicked into gear, mounting a defense by pointing out her ingratitude: "Don't you know how many people would kill to live in the greatest city in the world, *right* across from Dylan's Candy Bar?!"[9] Defensiveness of this kind, it turns out, does not make for marital harmony. I was desperate to maintain my own righteousness, and I did so by foisting the blame on her, suggesting that the real issue had to do with her lack of perspective.

Ten years down the line, my cheeks still redden in embarrassment. I wasn't just married to her; I was married to an idea of myself as a responsible guy and budding provider. Yet our predicament contradicted that image 100 percent, causing more than a little internal dissonance. To diminish that dissonance, I attempted to justify my actions, casting my (then pregnant!) wife as the problem to bolster my own sinking self-regard. That the tactic royally backfired probably goes without saying. Self-justification put us at odds when what we needed was to band together. It made a bad situation worse.

Thankfully, every now and then something would puncture my self-righteousness—the entire building shaking, for instance— my facade would collapse, and we'd laugh about how ridiculous it all was. Thank God I married a forgiving woman with a great sense of humor. She understood the truism to which I only paid lip service, "It's better to be kind than right." For love to blossom, our inner accountants need to be laid off.

Yet rare is the romantic relationship—or really any kind of relationship—that doesn't keep a record of wrongs. Maybe that's why 1 Corinthians remains such a wedding staple. We go to the altar to answer, publicly and definitively, that our beloved is more than enough—they for us, and we for them. The very next

---

9. Judging by how long it took the landlords to fill the apartment upstairs, the answer was: not many.

day, our bedroom becomes the courtroom where that verdict is re-tried.

It would be one thing if such scorekeeping worked, but it never has and never will, not where the heart is concerned. When one person's gain equals the other's loss, the relationship between them always suffers. We become competitors rather than teammates.

Moreover, like a husband pointing out the dishes he's done in order to leverage some gratitude from his wife, the second we harness our good deeds for credit is the second they become less good. All of a sudden, a price tag is dangling off of what was supposed to be a gift. "If I knew that you'd require a ton of affirmation and thanks, or that you'd hold it over my head, I would've done the dishes myself!" And that's just the petty stuff.

The language of scorekeeping is the language of conditionality. "I'll do this for you because you do that for me." "I'll hold up my end of the bargain as long as you hold up yours," we say. However egalitarian our intention, that kind of nonassurance sets us up for a life of accounting. But what works at the office runs out of gas at home.

An I-did-this-for-you-so-now-you-do-that-for-me stance can be downright manipulative, a way of controlling the other person and getting them to do what we want. It can also convey distrust, as though we wouldn't willingly do X, Y, or Z for our significant other without coercion. If I feel that you're trying to change me, I will resist, or hide. Whereas if I feel loved just as I am, in my hurt and neurosis and neediness, well, then I find myself wanting to be more pleasant, generous—and easier to deal with, especially in relation to *your* neurosis and need!

Relationships characterized by credit-seeking and conditionality, in which we justify ourselves both to and at the expense of our partner, tend to bite the dust. In their book *Mistakes Were Made (But Not by Me)*, social psychologists Carol Tavris and Elliot Aronson describe how a fixation on righteousness can choke the life out of love:

> The vast majority of couples who drift apart do so slowly, over time, in a snowballing pattern of blame and self-justification. Each partner focuses on what the other one is doing wrong, while justifying his or her own preferences, attitudes, and ways of doing things. . . . From our standpoint, therefore, misunderstandings, conflicts, personality differences, and even angry quarrels are not the assassins of love; self-justification is.

We always lose when we keep score. No one wins when we play the blame game. Whatever cliché you prefer, the truth is plain: self-justification and love don't mix, not over the long haul. Love, at its core, transcends emotional bartering. It cannot flourish when one or both parties feel like they're always playing catch-up or in danger of getting fired.

An Aside about Sex

When it comes to the meeting of needs in a relationship, no space plays a more prominent role than the bedroom. Sex all too often functions as a bargaining chip between lovers, something earned (or taken) rather than given, a reward-punishment mechanism, and therefore a major source of blame and resentment.

However, you don't have to be in a committed relationship, or even sexually active, to be familiar with scorekeeping and performancism as it relates to sex. If a traditionally religious point of view is preoccupied with the perils of sexual promiscuity, a secular mindset is similarly concerned with the perils of chastity. In the wake of the sexual revolution of the late 1960s and '70s, sexual expression came to be held as virtually synonymous with self-expression, an unquestioned good and therefore measure of enoughness. We are no longer justified by our sexual purity so much as our sexual *appeal*.

It's true: today, sexlessness is far more stigmatized and shameful than its opposite. Take celebrities, our modern-day aristocracy. The same gossip magazines that cover the royals so tenaciously also spotlight Hollywood's latest and greatest because both groups embody righteousness in the public eye. They comprise the two most popular human-sized channels for our aspirations. It's just that what sets celebrities apart—what marks them as highly favored and holy—isn't lineage so much as sex appeal (and, occasionally, talent).

Such a context naturally marginalizes virgins rather than applauding or encouraging them, whilst attitudes that diminish sex or simply promote libidinal constraint are branded heretical and even dangerous. As essayist Mark Greif observes, "One of the cruel betrayals of sexual liberation, in liberalization, was the illusion that the person can be free only if he holds sex as all-important and exposes it endlessly to others—providing it, proving it, enjoying it." In other words, when it comes to sex, we may have traded one piety for another.

A staunchly performancist culture goes one step further. Sex serves as another arena in which to distinguish ourselves, to assert our prowess and significance, to build ourselves up rather than give ourselves away. Who we're sleeping with, and how often, correlates directly to our overall score in the game of life.

We witness this tendency on college campuses perhaps most of all. Having spent the last ten years working with American undergraduates, I'm convinced that what some observers have mistaken for a hedonistic hook-up culture among college students is actually a fresh annex of performancism.

Exhibit A would have to be the institution at Yale University known as Sex Week. Every two years, students in New Haven gather for an array of adult product "demonstrations" and presentations by pornographers and sex therapists. What looks on the surface to be a celebration of self-indulgence and shock-my-parents rebellion may be less transgressive than it appears. Back in 2010, one female attendee of a Sex Week event called "Getting What You Really Want" surfaced part of the motivation when she told the *Yale Daily News*, "Many of us here have never failed at anything, and we don't want to start now."

In this way, sex becomes one more column in which to excel, an opportunity not just to connect but impress, to garner admiration according to one's accomplishments or conquests. Instead of labeling events like Sex Week evidence of unshackled indulgence, it might be more accurate to view them as a measure of just how tightly these students are shackled to their performancism and haunted by their fears of not-enoughness.

Then again, it may be that young people just really, really like sex.

The Soulmate Myth

Romantic love captures our devotion for good reason: it is the closest most of us will get to transcendence in this life and, as such, is the single best approximation of salvation available to the human creature. The exalted language we employ to extol romantic love fits. We call it enchanting, uplifting, sublime, heavenly, everything and more; anyone who has experienced it firsthand knows those terms fail to do the real thing justice.

The hope here is not to denigrate romantic love—not remotely!—so much as preserve its magic. The more pressure we put on our relationships to provide transcendence, the less they will be able to deliver.

Nowhere do we see romance cast as salvation more overtly than in the widespread notion that there's one special someone out there for each of us, the yin to our yang, a single person who holds the key to both our personal happiness and ultimate fulfillment. As Saint Jerry of Maguire famously opines to his estranged wife, "You. Complete. Me." The doctrine he was drawing upon is what we might semi-affectionately term the Soulmate Myth.

The Soulmate Myth has become so engrained in our thinking that we hardly notice it anymore. When a new relationship is going well, we tell our friends, "I think she may be *the one!*" Wedding toasts invariably describe the couple as "meant to be."

The Soulmate Myth takes root well before we enter the dating pool and can persist long after we've settled down. In one of her popular Ask Polly advice columns, Heather Havrilesky captures the innate religiosity well:

> For years, I turned distracted dudes into demigods using only the powers of my own imagination. . . . That was my art, my practice: putting arbitrary guys on a pedestal and then painting a rich and elaborate backdrop behind them, and then praying to that vision day after day after day. . . . As long as he wasn't a real person, he'd never ruin my vivid creations.

She nails the tendency—by no means limited to women—to look to another person to provide for us what we cannot provide ourselves: not just validation but redemption. In pursuit of freedom from the nagging suspicion that we're not enough, we turn those around us into potential solutions to be leveraged rather than human beings to be loved.

Seldom do we willingly or consciously elect to view others this way. But such is the allure of the Soulmate Myth that it tends to linger in the back of our minds whether we want it to or not. Like most religious frameworks, it speaks to our deepest longings and fears, below the level of rational decision-making.

Hollywood has long milked the Soulmate Myth for ticket sales. It makes for great drama, elevating otherwise quotidian dating escapades into epic quests to fulfill one's destiny. It turns our lives into movies, transforming humdrum days into something far more flattering and exciting. We get to star in our own personal Nicholas Sparks flick, where our neuroses magically morph into quirks and all sorts of shady actions become instantly justifiable, even laudable.

This is not to suggest that the seculosity of romance can be neatly laid at the feet of tinsel town, or Hallmark, or even America itself. A quick survey of recent history reveals deeper roots.

Like a Horse and Carriage?

By any measure, the past couple hundred years have witnessed an enormous shift in what we look for in a spouse. Our expectations of relationships, and by extension one another, have escalated dramatically.

For most of human history, people paired off for pragmatic and economic reasons: for land, peace, security, offspring, survival. It's not that love was never a consideration, just that it was one of many, and rarely the most important. Experts refer to this model as "a marriage of reason." Think *Game of Thrones*.

As a result of factors too varied to enumerate here, that model was supplemented and eventually replaced by a new one, the so-called "marriage of instinct" in which attraction and desire drive us to the altar.[10] We now privilege sentiment over strategy, instinct over prudence. Think *The Bachelor*.

This does not mean logistics don't play a role in who we end up with—or that people don't marry for money anymore!—just that those concerns usually come second. Where once we sought someone to meet our material and societal needs, today we seek someone to meet our emotional needs.

Or so the story goes.

Upon closer examination, it could be that we haven't switched models so much as combined them. Renowned marriage therapist Esther Perel characterized the arrangement this way:

> We come to one person, and we basically are asking them to give us what once an entire village used to provide: give me belonging, give me identity, give me continuity, but give me transcendence and mystery and awe all in one. Give me comfort, give me edge. Give me novelty, give me familiarity. Give me predictability, give me surprise.

---

10. For example, movements like Romanticism, which were responding to the (French) Enlightenment's overemphasis on reason.

Sub out "an entire village" for "God" and the truth of what we are actually looking for comes into focus. We want to marry a savior.

The irony is worth taking a moment to absorb: under the auspices of the secular, you could hardly formulate a *more* religious definition of marriage or romance than the supposedly secular one Perel describes.

To the extent that her diagnosis holds true, we are not giving our potential partner a tall order so much as an impossible one. Which of us could even come close to filling the position? The very attempt necessitates delusion. Meaning, the magnitude of what we're hoping to receive from our spouse—everything—outweighs what we ourselves can offer to an alarming extent. Whoever we marry within such a framework will fail us—and we them—simply by virtue of them being a person.

Come to find out, ratcheting up our expectations of one another tends not to produce a ratcheted-up response. As the sages of Alcoholics Anonymous say, "expectation is a planned resentment," and there are no greater expectations than the astronomic ones we foist on a potential (soul)mate, acknowledged or not. As Becker warns, "If your partner is your 'All' then any shortcoming in him becomes a major threat to you." If we get married expecting the other person to be our everything, we set ourselves up for pain if not scorn.

I know this from personal experience.

When Every Day Is Opposite Day

A few months after my wife and I got engaged, an older friend of hers pulled me aside and tried to do me a favor. He told me that if there was anything he wished he could have told his premarital self, it was that, no matter who you marry, their way of doing things will be the opposite of yours. If he had known that beforehand, it might have spared him and his sweetheart considerable heartache.

Like much of what people tell you before you tie the knot or have kids, his words were both 100 percent true and 100 percent impossible to understand on the front end of the experience. I was intrigued but baffled.

To the outside eye, my wife and I were coming from embarrassingly similar places: both of us had grown up in or around big cities on the East Coast of the United States, north of the Mason-Dixon line. We had both been baptized in the same type of church, both sets of parents were still married, both of us were raised with siblings of the same sex and, among our peers, we were both fish out of water on the Jesus question. We enjoyed the same movies and appreciated the same jokes. Sure, we weren't identical, but opposites? No way. We were what wedding magazines call "well matched"—who knows, maybe even soulmates.

And yet, her friend was right. In the life of a romantic relationship, similarities are largely taken for granted. Where you get bogged down—where you *live*—are the places of difference. It doesn't matter how minor those differences appear to be. The tiniest points of friction will come to occupy disproportionately vast emotional space, so much so that it often *feels* like you're coming from 180-degree opposing vantage points. You and your spouse may hold 95 percent of life and outlook in common; the other 5 percent is where your relationship is going to take place.

In other words, however congruently the two of you stack up on paper, you won't feel well matched. You won't feel like soulmates. Not when it matters.

No doubt this explains why the most popular *New York Times* article of 2016 had nothing to do with the presidential election. In a year overfull with controversy, the headline that garnered the largest audience was "Why You Will Marry the Wrong Person," by philosopher Alain de Botton. Not why you *might* marry the wrong person, but why you *will.*

What sounds like a pessimistic angle struck a massive chord, well beyond the regular readership of America's paper of record. It did so because it surfaced the seculosity of romance that occupies so much of the relational landscape today. De Botton put his finger on the extent to which we have, often without realizing it, made potential mates into potential saviors and the fallout that pressure creates in our hearts and lives.

At first glance, plenty of relationships do not appear to fit this mold. Maybe the person we're dating is all too human—"not in the same league"—and that's part of what makes it work. The whole point is that they *don't* make us feel bad about ourselves or remind us of our not-enoughness. Or maybe we seek out rocky relationships with clearly flawed or even damaged individuals because we find the drama exciting.

In those cases, it could be that we are relying less on the person themselves than the goods they provide—namely, how they make us feel. In their presence we feel un-depressed instead of numb, alive instead of deadened. Maybe it doesn't matter so much that they make us feel good or bad, what's important is the *magnitude* of the emotion. It must be large enough to crowd out—to save us from—other unpleasantness and emptiness. Seculosity all the way around.

Maximize My Love

While the whole star-crossed-lovers thing has been around since time immemorial, the anxiety surrounding it only exploded recently.

One word accounts for the mushrooming, and it rhymes with "schminternet." In his surprisingly trenchant book *Modern Romance*, comedian, writer, and cautionary tale Aziz Ansari explained the situation in terms of *maximizing*: "[The internet] doesn't simply help us find the best thing out there; it has helped to produce the idea that there *is* a best thing and, if we search hard enough, we can find it."[11]

Ansari contrasts his generation with that of his parents, who seem happy together despite being the product of an arranged marriage. In decades past, he explains, one's potential mates consisted primarily of the young people in one's neighborhood or town. Rather than a soulmate, you looked for someone who was "good enough." Anything better than a total disaster could be viewed as a win.

The situation grew exponentially more complicated—and fraught—once technology opened up the field of possible partners first to everyone in the country and then to, well, everyone on the planet. As a result, today's generation faces a pressure to find the

---

11. The Ansari reference isn't random. In the church of seculosity, stand-up comedians (and late-night talk-show hosts) are the preachers.

"perfect person." Anything less than that, we're told, is settling. Dating in this light becomes a highly protracted and agonizing process: get it right, or else.

Much like when we tell college graduates to follow their dreams, the fruit of such singular pressure is second-guessing and self-consciousness rather than clarity and gratification. "She's warm and caring, but her family sure could be easier," we hear ourselves comment. "He's sweet and honest, but there might be a guy out there who's sweet, honest, *and* on more secure financial footing." We start to sound like Jerry Seinfeld in his fabled sitcom, whose insistence on foible-free flawlessness in a woman—on snagging Ms. Right—ensures that he ends up alone.[12]

This holds true within a committed relationship just as much as in the lead-up to one. Perel goes so far as to say, "We don't divorce—or have affairs—because we are unhappy, but because we could be happier." From a scorekeeping point of view, our current romantic tally may be respectable, but we can't shake the suspicion that if we rolled the dice again, it could be higher. It's not that real connection and contentment don't exist, but our own insistence on maximization in all things has a curious way of backfiring.

The shadow-side of the Soulmate Myth should be fairly obvious at this point. Heaven help you if you don't find "the one"—or find them too late. You have not just failed at dating, but life. When salvation itself waits at the top of the Empire State Building for you to "meet cute," you better hope you don't get caught in traffic.

But say you *have* found someone who is all those things, who may in fact be your soulmate—you better not let them slip away!

---

12. Not that I'd want to be married to a close-talker or a lady with man-hands.

You better not let them see you for who you really are, capable of both beauty *and* cheapness, warmth *and* spite. All of a sudden, vulnerability, impropriety, and all those other unsavory things that are part of knowing—and therefore loving—another flesh-and-blood human have been outlawed from the equation.

Long story short, pursuing love in an atmosphere of acute seculosity seems to preclude love being found at all.

Love Actually

What does romance on the other side of seculosity look like? Perhaps it looks a bit like Molly Howes's second marriage.

Six years after a painful divorce, Molly met Peter. She was, by her own admission, cynical about love and especially the altar-bound kind. Peter's first wife had died, and he fell hard for Molly, countering her doubts with relentless optimism and promising all manner of bliss and security. Their relationship would be different from the ones she had known. Their families would integrate. They would have more than enough money. He would make everything all right.

Eventually, Peter won Molly over and they got married. But you can probably guess what happened next. All did not transpire as Peter had predicted. His son refused to talk to Molly. They accrued debt.

Molly confesses that in the past, when disappointment like this had reared its head, she would do one of three things: (1) bail on the relationship, (2) stick with it but blame the man forever, or (3) stick with it and blame herself.

She recalls the night that things came to a head. They were unpacking their bags after a visit with his family, and she was lamenting his kids' continued resistance to her. Peter dropped the clothes he was holding and under his breath muttered, "I can't take it anymore. It's too much for me. I know I said I wanted us to talk about everything, that I wanted to know everything you felt. But I can't handle it. I'm sorry."

In the thick silence that followed, Molly finished putting away the laundry. Peter went downstairs. She got in the shower, turned on the water, and sat on the tiled floor in grief and disbelief.

You might think that was the end of Peter and Molly. But it wasn't. She writes:

> I still wonder why the disappointments didn't doom our relationship, but now, eight years later, I think our real relationship began with them. In the aftermath, something new happened: He had let me down, and he cared about my reaction. I didn't have to pretend that the falling bricks didn't hurt. . . . That's why he's a good person for me: I can dream a little myself and, if the dreams don't come true, I'm not left alone to pick up the pieces.

Painful as it was, the death of their expectations birthed something beautiful, something akin to real love. Instead of "I love you as long as you don't disappoint me" their relationship took on a new operating philosophy: "I love you *in the midst* of our mutual disappointments."

To a lesser extent, their story is my own. My wife and I like to say that our marriage didn't actually begin until three years after our Big Day, after our illusions about one another (and ourselves) had been sufficiently deflated, and we stopped taking ourselves quite so seriously. Coincidentally, we also moved apartments.

What we learned—and what we still forget with astonishing frequency—is what Molly and Peter learned. Real love does not recoil at weakness. That is where it begins. Love without vulnerability is not really love at all. It's more like mutual objectification, where the other person serves as a canvas upon which we project not only our idealized selves but our spiritual and emotional yearnings.

Real love is not something we decide on. Nor is it something we earn. Love is more than something we fall into; it is something we *fail* into. What sounds like a somewhat more tragic view of life is actually a starting point for compassion, forgiveness, and joy. After all, we stand a better chance of loving our spouse (or neighbor) when we aren't looking to them to do or be what they cannot do or be.

Eye of the Beholder

I think this is close to what the apostle John meant when he spoke of God being love. The love of God, as we seen borne out in the life and death of Jesus Christ, seems to assume from the outset that we are all severely handicapped in our ability to love other people, let alone our Creator. And yet, like a shepherd going after a lost sheep, it persists. It does not insist on proof of lovability but produces it.

The Bible does not eschew romance or deny its transcendent thrill. Instead, it posits a third model for romance and marriage, not one of expediency or mutual gratification but of self-emptying and sacrifice: a model in which the groom gives himself fully for his wayward bride, satisfying rather than introducing expectations, the sign of his fidelity being not a ring but a cross.

This groom, Jesus himself, is under no illusions about what he's getting/gotten himself into. He does not wait for his beloved to get her feelings right in order to leverage his devotion, but stands ready to absolve her of them. He knows that he's marrying the wrong person, that "the wrong people" are all there are. Yet he refuses to spare himself the heartache.

I am not suggesting that any of us are Jesus—or are married to Jesus, or should hammer nails into our spouse. God forbid! The point is that the relationships we are given to enjoy in the here and now, to the extent that they're sustaining, are pursued *from* the vantage point of assurance not *for* it. "Compatibility is an achievement of love. It must not be its precondition."

To break things down into theological language, which is ultimately the language of love, the Law commands that we love perfectly. The Gospel announces that we are perfectly loved. Or to put it more colloquially, the Soulmate Myth commands that we be perfectly loved. Grace announces that we already are.

At the heart of true romance lies acceptance, not challenge.[13] Once the defining *Yes* has been uttered and the proving project can be laid to rest, if only for a moment, love blooms. Once the sweatpants come out, you might say, and we catch a glimpse of what my father, Paul Zahl, describes in *Grace in Practice*:

> I was human with this person, and instead of turning away from me . . . this person turned toward me. . . . It had nothing to do with my worthiness. It was love in my direction from

---

13. Let us not forget Heather Havrilesky's classic formulation: "True romance [is] like the movie *True Romance*: Two deluded, lazy people face a bewildering sea of filth and blood and gore together, but they make it through somehow, some way, without losing their minds completely."

the eye of the beholder. . . . It was not sex per se or physical attraction in a vacuum. It was the underlying moment of truth coupled with belovedness that dazzled your life. The light of being loved, and loved in your humanity as opposed to ideality, was the inaugurating sun of this particular system.

Maybe you remember a moment when you felt the same, when the truth about you was coupled with belovedness. These God-given moments are real and worth cherishing. They are worth going back to whenever the wires get crossed and ill feeling descends. Not merely because they remind us of our love for one another but because of the picture they give us of God's gracious disposition toward people sunk in relational failure, crippled by resentment, and stalked by loneliness. Whether you're married or divorced, dating or single, that disposition never changes.

To be sure, even the most well-matched partner will let us down, and we them. Another person cannot give us what we need, and much of our dissatisfaction stems from the fact that we continue to believe that they can and should. I cannot help but wonder—and pray for—what it would look like to believe that Someone already has.

CHAPTER 3

THE SECULOSITY
OF PARENTING

T here we were, him holding his newborn son and me with my two-year-old clinging to my legs. We were talking, as men do these days, about baby books, and I was trying to remember the last two of the "Five S's." I had Swing, Swaddle, and Shush, but couldn't for the life of me remember the others. (Note: Side and Suck.)

It was embarrassing. At the time of our conversation, my wife and I were cruising through month ninety of uninterrupted diaper life; babies had been our modus operandi for what felt like forever. I should've had the lingo down cold. My buddy *should* have been marveling at my effortless Dad skills. But whatever nook of my brain held those words had been, ahem, wiped clean.

When someone mentioned the phrase "1-2-3 Magic" a couple days later, it took me a full minute to register what they were talking about: a discipline system for young children, popular among my peers, and briefly implemented in our house. By "briefly," I mean a single afternoon.

Like many new parents, my wife and I devoured a stack of books on parenting before our first child was born. Some of these we bought ourselves, but most were given to us by friends. It's a long nine months that first time around, and the uncertainty of what's about to happen looms large. After the initial shock wears off, the realization slowly dawns that everything is about to change, and you spend the remainder of the pregnancy pinballing between excitement, trepidation, tedium, and terror. It's good preparation for what comes next.

Truth be told, I cannot remember a single thing I learned from a parenting book. I wish I was exaggerating. I can remember tips that friends offered and stories our own parents told, but all the approaches and to-do's we absorbed vanished the second our little guy came into the world.

This doesn't mean the books didn't serve a purpose. They served what may have been their *true* purpose: to assuage our anxiety. Under the guise of providing guidance and relaying the latest science, what we read helped us feel a little less of afraid of what we were getting into. They painted a picture of cause-and-effect that calmed us. If the baby wouldn't sleep, we could try one of eight sleep-training methods. If the baby had trouble eating, we had a list of products proven to ease the process.

It doesn't take a private eye to notice how much the parenting section in the bookstore resembles the religious one, often self-consciously. How to raise a happy child, a gritty child, a child who reads, a creative child, a kind child—these handbooks strike a very similar tone and adopt an almost identical format to Christian ones on prayer, grief, purpose, evangelism, or church growth.

In lieu of denominations, however, you have *camps*. During our tour of duty, the two dominant camps went by the names

Babywise and Attachment. The Babywise books counseled putting your infant on a strict schedule of naps and feeding in order to ensure their flourishing. The parent knows best, and a reliable structure will give the child a deep sense of security as they develop and grow. Since all newborn homo sapiens have the roughly same needs for food and sleep and love, this top-down strategy works across the board, the Babywise claim.

The Attachment paradigm, on the other hand, counseled a bottom-up approach in which the parent pays close attention to the child, following the child's lead when it comes to the rhythms of sleeping and eating. Paramount is the child's attachment to the mother, the bond from which all other health derives. Contrary to the Babywise approach, the Attachment child falls asleep when they're tired, weans themselves off the breast when they're ready, sleeps next to the parent until they ask for their own bed, and so forth. It sounds like less effort, certainly less coercion. Come to find out, attempting to raise a child in accordance with one's instincts isn't automatically more relaxing than trying to make them comply with a schedule, since you're liable to find yourself constantly questioning whether or not you're following your instincts faithfully enough.

While ostensibly opposite, both camps—and the many that fall on the continuum between them—project a vision of right-minded child-rearing that is as exclusive and conformist as anything in the 1950s. Both camps have their codes of conduct, both have their cardinal sins.

No matter where an expert falls on the continuum, their manual gives us the sense that there are things we can do, that we have some power, that it isn't all blind instinct. I recall a female friend wondering aloud before she had kids, "How do I know if I'll be maternal?" You can't, I remember thinking (to myself!).

The Parenting-Industrial Complex

Babies are one thing, actual child-rearing another. Few subjects provoke more anxiety in our culture than raising kids. The responsibility and mystery a child represents leads all but the most self-assured to grasp for any foothold of control they can find, any means to reduce the unknowns and gain some peace of mind.

A quick perusal of the baby department on Amazon belies a related truth: no one ever went broke catering to (American) parental anxiety. When the word *parent* made its transition sometime in the early 1980s from noun to verb, it birthed(!) a parenting-industrial complex that has yet to slow its expansion. I'm not just talking about books and magazines and websites, but conferences, seminars, podcasts, schools, medications, therapies, tutors, and college admissions prep courses. The deluge of parenting resources corresponds more or less directly to the size of our fears, which previous generations would likely classify as paranoia.

Neurosis isn't the only reason we focus so much energy on our children these days, though. Thanks to the advent of developmental psychology, we are more aware than ever of how crucial those early years are. We know, often from firsthand experience, that the wounds inflicted and inadequacies internalized during childhood can trail a person well into adulthood. Moreover, a fire hydrant–strength stream of internet articles ensures that no potential risk to our children goes unreported. Even if we have the wherewithal to ignore the endless feed of "studies show," we love our kids and are eager to know how best to shepherd them.

The emotional premium, combined with the surplus of data and obvious financial opportunity, means that parents today are bombarded with competing and often conflicting techniques, all of which promise superstar offspring if only you follow their advice. Most of these schools of thought position themselves not just as wise or helpful but right, even right*eous.*

Rarely does a month go by without some fresh parenting trend making headlines and, with it, ringing some fresh alarm bell about all the ways we are ruining our kids. If your kids are picky eaters, you might want to check out a book on French parenting. If they seem a bit risk-averse or hooked on screens, you should probably watch a documentary about Norwegian kindergartens. Your fourth-grader's suffering from a lack of motivation? I hear Sheryl Sandberg has a new podcast out.

The New Yorker parodied this reality hilariously in a satirical report, "A recent study has shown that if American parents read one more long-form think piece about parenting they will go [f-%$&*] ape shit." Which is another way of saying that the more opinions we absorb about how to parent well, the more expectations we find that we—and our children—are failing to meet and the more ways in which we discover we are doing it wrong.

The net result of the parenting-industrial complex is not a pacifying of mom and dad's anxiety but its multiplication.

I remember waking in a panic one morning after reading an article about how toddlers should be read to for at least an hour a day. We read books before bed, but a full hour? No way. The rest of that day, instead of actually listening to my kids, every interchange turned into an evaluation of their linguistic development, my obvious disappointment in their less-than-impressive vocabularies matched only by the festival of recrimination going on in my head. When evening rolled around, I announced the new hour-long story-time policy, thus adding an element of stress to what was supposed to be their wind-down period. Needless to say, the whole situation proved so exhausting that I fell asleep ten minutes in, only to be awoken a couple hours later by my oldest son, who was having a nightmare about me being mad at him.

My Child Is an Honor Student

The outsized anxiety should tip us off that the well-being of our children isn't the only thing at stake. Wherever the line between an overdeveloped sense of parental responsibility and full-blown seculosity lies, we appear to have crossed it.

A recent cartoon spells out the situation brilliantly. A mother and father sit with their elementary-aged son in a waiting room. The closed door next to their couch reads "Admissions." The mother looks actively concerned, her eyebrows raised in attention, her face unsmiling. Meanwhile, the father leans over and says to the boy, "Now, remember, be the yourself we talked about."

An admissions interview for someone whose feet don't yet touch the ground—the set-up alone underlines the absurdity of our cultural performancism. A pressure to prove oneself that, in the not-so-distant past, would have been reserved for those entering university or the workforce is now aimed at preteens. The closed door signifies the external pressure, and then there's the internal kind inherent in the father's twisting the "just be yourself" self-acceptance mantra into something wryly opposite.

Parental overinvestment pervades the scene, evidenced by the fact that both are present in the first place. The parents, you see, are on trial just as much as the boy. The forthcoming judgment on their son constitutes a vicarious one on them. You could even say that their own enoughness hangs in the balance *more* than that of their boy, who, if not too young to know what's going on, is certainly too young to take real responsibility for his performance. Which is why he appears so much less nervous than his folks.

The most overt, and probably most damaging, expression of the seculosity of parenting occurs when parents lean on their children for their enoughness. A common emblem of this attitude would be the popular bumper sticker that reads "My Child Is an Honor Student at _____ Elementary School." Something meant to express pride in one's child serves a convenient double purpose, signaling parental virtue, as evidenced by the gag response sticker "You're Kid's an Honor Student—But You're a Moron." As the kids get older, those stickers are replaced with logos of their college in the parents' back windshield. The message to other parents is clear: I am enough because my child goes to *this* college.

That's just one small, relatively innocuous example. But it points to the larger and less benign trend known as helicopter parenting, an unflattering label that refers to the propellered vehicle's propensity for hovering. A close cousin of the helicopter parent— its latest (d)evolution, at least—would be the bulldozer parent, who knocks down any obstacle in their child's path.[14]

Black Hawk Down

Talk to your local middle-school English teacher or soccer coach, and they'll regale you with tales of moms and dads whose concern for their child has inspired a hands-on parenting approach that borders on maniacal. I'm not just talking about parents who voice their every complaint, but those who complete their children's

---

14. *Lawnmower parenting* is another term for basically the same thing, the lesson being that, once again, heavy machinery + small children = bad news.

homework for them, run their student-council campaigns, write their college essays. It's much more common than you'd think. There's even an off-kilter logic to it: if the kid's grade is indeed a referendum on the parents, they might as well bypass the middleman and take the test themselves.

Talk to the parents themselves, though, and they'll rarely boast about their overinvolvement. Most of them feel forced into it by the college admissions arms race, the ultimate measure of (upper-) middle-class righteousness. Even parents who would like to opt out of the rabid protectiveness feel locked into it as a consequence of their own children having to compete for spots.

If there's an unspoken mandate at work in the performancist parenting paradigm, it has to do with upward mobility. Good parents do everything in their power to ensure their child "gets further" than them on the socioeconomic ladder—or at minimum that they don't demote the family somehow. Call it the doctrine of filial advancement. Adam Strassberg, a psychiatrist and the father of two teenagers in affluent Palo Alto, commented that while many of the parents in his community are "wealthy and secure beyond imagining," they're consumed by fear of losing their station or failing to pass it on to their kids. "Maintaining and advancing insidiously high educational standards in our children is a way to soothe this anxiety."

Reason doesn't play much of a role here, which is ironic, since education is the apparent motivation.

To be fair, while visions of future success—or fears of future destitution—fuel a good deal of helicopter and bulldozer behavior, not all of it runs on an engine of naked ambition. Some portion involves a desire to shield our child from unpleasantness and pain.

Whatever the motivation, helicopter parenting is an inherently religious undertaking, not only in how the child's achievement becomes the parent's justifying story but in how it plays to our divine aspirations. Human mothers and fathers take on the role of the all-knowing, all-seeing, all-protecting Parent.

The thinking makes sense: if we're not there for our children when they're alone or confused or frightened or hurting, who will be? Whatever creed we claim to follow, hovering behavior betrays a belief that there is no future for our kids—ultimately no enoughness—beyond that which we engineer for them. Such astronomical burden is a recipe for breakdown in parents just as much as their teenage kids.

If helicopter parenting were *really* all about safeguarding our kids—rather than propping up our own righteousness—then we would stop when it became clear that it was not helping but actively harming them. No baby learns to walk without falling down a lot. A good parent even allows them to fall, over and over again. There's evidence that children who are never exposed to dirt fail to develop an adequate immune system. We forget that the same holds true for other aspects of life. Those who have never experienced failure lack resilience, sometimes fatally so. Protectiveness does not always protect.

The fallout of performancism-based helicopter parenting has taken on increasingly devastating dimensions in recent years. A high-school teacher in a suburb west of Chicago maintains that "the number of advanced-placement classes that local students feel compelled to take and the number of hospitalizations for depression rise in tandem." While we must be careful not to draw a one-to-one correlation between mental illness and meritocracy—the reality is far more complicated—to deny any relationship between the two would be naïve. Former Stanford dean Julie Lythcott-Haims puts it this way:

When parents have tended to do the stuff of life for kids—
the waking up, the transporting, the reminding about deadlines and obligations, the bill-paying, the question-asking,
the decision-making, the responsibility-taking, the talking to
strangers, and the confronting of authorities, kids may be in
for quite a shock when parents turn them loose in the world
of college or work. They will experience setbacks, which will
feel to them like failure.

Everyday reversals that appear petty to outsiders take on an epic
emotional scope according to their novelty. The more that parents
succeed in building the perfect world for their child, the more the
child will feel like a failure when she can't build one for herself. Put
differently, "spoiling" a kid doesn't just mean giving them everything they want but—like dirt and the immune system—means
failing to inoculate them against failure.

Instead of preparing kids for a glorious future, parental overinvolvement produces a fragility in our offspring that makes them
ripe for crisis. A parent's omnipresence may even convey a crushing message of its own: that despite all the cheerleading, the child
is incapable of fending for themselves.

The Eye of a Tiger (Mom)

If helicopter parenting is the grown-up version of the Attachment
camp, then the grown-up variation on Babywise is tiger parenting.
Infamously popularized by Yale law professor Amy Chua, tiger
parenting refers to the anti-coddling style favored by many Asian
households in which young children keep to strictly regimented
schedules, and shame is openly employed as a motivating tool. If

you do not get good grades, the child is told, you will bring shame not only to yourself but your family. Enjoyment never really enters the equation. Chua writes:

A lot of parents today are terrified that something they say to their children might make them "feel bad." But, hey, if they've done something wrong, they should feel bad. Kids with a sense of responsibility, not entitlement, who know when to experience gratitude and humility, will be better at navigating the social shoals of college.

That such an approach would encounter some friction with a Western audience should come as no surprise. In response to criticism, Chua defended her approach by pointing to both dependably high test scores and hard-working children who did not fall apart at the slightest setback. She argued that a more hands-off approach instilled confidence by communicating to the child that they were perfectly adept on their own. In this way, tiger parenting represents the opposite of helicopter parenting.

What a child really needs, according to Chua, is not for the parent to stand over him but against him, reinforcing the voice of performancist accusation. In practice, this looks like tough love all the way, especially during the years when a child is most apt to internalize it. And while it may get results, Chua underestimates how much the self-justifying parent will use the it's-good-for-them as license for all their most dictatorial impulses. A joyless enterprise, no matter how you cut it, and one that makes zero room for compulsion on the part of the child *or* parent.[15]

---

15. I would hate to read her book on marriage.

Weighing the relative merits of each approach lies beyond our purview, at least when it comes to the child themselves. What both helicopter and tiger parenting have in common, however, is their unquestioned performancism. Both are fundamentally future-focused and, as such, posit achievement as the yardstick of human worth.

Before we go further, let us resist the temptation to turn these observations into another accusation of parental misfire or a question of blame. Instead, let the record show that our kids' self-justifying impulses predate their indoctrination into whatever form of performancism we've elected to pursue. Just last week I overheard an introduction between two three-year-olds where, instead of leading with their names, one informed the other that he was taller. It was downhill from there.

First Glimmer of Light

By way of counterexample, one image that has helped me is that of Paul Westerberg, lead singer and songwriter of The Replacements, Minneapolis's notorious rock band. Despite their penchant for self-sabotage, the band made some waves in the 1980s, especially in college circles, spawning a cult who couldn't get enough of their ramshackle charm and Paul's heart-on-sleeve poetics.

After his father died in 2004, long after the band broke up, Paul eulogized the man in song. The track "My Dad" included a telling bit of trivia: the fact that his father never saw him play a concert. Such an admission might imply a lack of love, but to Paul, it was the opposite. He remarked to an interviewer at the time:

> I've always maintained—and I still do to this day—I'm perfectly fine that [my father] never came to my office and

watched me work, you know? It kept it pure that I was his son, that I was no more than the little boy he played catch with, who now plays catch with his son.

What an incredible thing to say. So many father-son relationships, even the good ones, contain an element of proving. Doubtless theirs did too, in other ways. Yet that's not what came across to Paul. What came across is that his father loved him apart from his fame or his achievements—he got "a kick out of seeing the family name in the newspaper," but that's all. Perhaps Paul couldn't possibly be more to his father than he already was: a living, breathing son, rather than a character in his father's justifying story.

The vignette points beyond itself to a paradigm in which the parent doesn't rely on the child for their own enoughness but gifts it to them, willy-nilly.

Are You a Good (Enough) Parent?

The seculosity of parenting exists *among* parents even more than between parents and children. We parents concern ourselves not just with how our kids stack up against other kids but with how we stack up against other parents and the parenting ideals we hold dear. Are we getting it right? Or at least *more* right than the family next door?

The quest for righteous parenting can be grueling. We start to worry less about the dangers posed to our children and more about what other parents *might* think about our parenting decisions. My friend Sarah writes about the barrage of judgment she faces daily from other mothers, both online and in person. "Questions about vegetable intake, academic rigor, and quality time lead us from one anxious moment to the next." These questions, however well meaning, turn into referenda on our parenting performance with remarkable velocity, the implication being that if we're not up on the latest info, we care less than those who are. And since there's always a new study or think piece to absorb, no one ever reaches the destination of enlightened parenting. A marketer's dream come true.

This cycle of not-enoughness is especially alluring to moms and dads who have no idea what they're doing, which is pretty much all of us. But even those who are overwhelmed by the perplexity of child-rearing can agree that no child benefits from a parent who's a nervous wreck all the time.

One response to intra-parental scrutiny is to up your game by curating your image more assiduously, managing others' perceptions as best you can (and exhausting yourself further in the process). This may work for a little while, but when it proves impossible you find yourself giving up and resenting the entire enterprise, and maybe even your children.

Another fashionable response involves publicly owning your failures as a parent. Moms and dads compete to be the one most behind the ball, "Oh, you forgot Susie's lunch money? Well, little Thomas hasn't had a bath in a week!" But this is just trading one form of self-justification—organization—for another: how comfortable we are with our shortcomings.

The third way of assuaging parental anxiety is something we've already touched on: we become enamored of a particular parenting philosophy and use it as a lens by which to sort those around us. If our neighbor's kid is acting out, it's because the parents have transgressed our code—have you *seen* how much screen time that boy gets?! Serves them right.

The appeal should be self-evident: a surefire parenting method offers us a modicum of control over the terrifying chaos of life. It grants its adherent agency, soothing fears about all that goes bump in the night. If I just find the best roadmap and possess the resolve to follow it, then I can effectively dictate outcomes, both for me and my child. Projecting order on the unruliness of the world to ease our troubled minds.[16]

Like religious doctrine, we seldom adopt a parenting method casually. Schools of parenting inspire denomination-like loyalty in which communities of like-minded parents function as de facto churches. Yet, the tighter we hold to our set of rules, the worse we feel when we fail to uphold them. We'll feel that much more defeated (and ashamed) when we bribe our kid with video games or lack the fortitude at the end of the day to deny *another* request for soda.[17]

No wonder the acrimony you encounter online over differences in parenting approaches can make the heat around political disagreements look tame. The implication is not just that you're a bad parent but a bad person, that if you're not in the right parenting camp, you aren't only cheating yourself but your children. The question, "What kind of a parent are you?" is shorthand for what kind of a person.

Yet every time we scrutinize another parent behind closed doors, we can rest assured we are being similarly scrutinized. Which is bad news, since none of us is the parent we intended to be. My friend Carrie describes a moment that every parent knows

---

16. Come to think of it, many an atheist would characterize Religion this way.

17. Purely hypothetical examples, of course. (Read: from the past twenty-four hours.)

all too well: when you say something to your child that you told yourself you'd never say to them, usually something that you were told as a child yourself, like, "Because I said so, that's why!" "If you behave today, I'll buy you whatever you want." "How could you do this to me?!" She writes:

All of those things I never imagined myself saying have stretched me out into a person I sometimes don't recognize. The mother-I-was-going-to-be wouldn't need much forgiveness, because she got it all right. Her kids ate her food, cheerfully, and never forgot a project or a deadline. She would keep her house tidy and lose all the baby weight in six weeks. The mother-I-was-going-to-be was going to be better than this. But the mother-I-was-going-to-be didn't need forgiveness because she doesn't exist. I think my husband and my kids are relieved that she doesn't.

Maybe our code is fixed like the Babywise/tiger camp, or maybe it fluctuates according to the individual, a la the Attachment/helicopter model. Whatever the case, the underlying appeal flows from the same source—control—as does the fruit, which is accusation and worry.

For here's the sad irony of every cult of control: what's meant to quell anxiety instead stimulates and even exacerbates it, regardless of intention. As recovering addicts often point out, "You cannot solve a problem with the same mindset you used to create it."

The truth is, there exists no single, definitively *right* way to parent. Which does not mean that all parenting advice is created equal—feeding/washing/holding your child regularly is better than the alternative, of that I am sure. But far too often the search for a single right technique only ends up creating added anxiety that we transmit to our children.

Whatever we may say we believe, the act of bringing a child into the world is fundamentally an act of faith, not control, and leaps of faith are scary. They often feel more like pushes. Yet however we get there, it's no coincidence that the freedom from control a newborn necessitates also ushers in love and joy.

Maybe becoming a parent is more of a *conversion* than an *evolution*. As much as folks can describe the experience, you don't know what you're getting into because you cannot know what you're getting into. Sure, you can account for all sorts of potential circumstances and problems related to the child, but you cannot account for the fact that you *yourself* will be a different person when the time comes.

There's so much law related to having a kid, and maybe that's the grace: the child itself, this beautiful rejoinder to our fondest strategies, this moment-to-moment reminder that our control only extends so far, this new person who makes us into a new person—one for whom the how-to's that once seemed so pressing fade into obsolescence and are replaced, however fleetingly, with a fresh MO, the only kind with the power to carry a person through the sleepless nights and endless demands ahead: the unconditional love of a parent for their writhing, exhausted offspring.

Love like this is the one thing no book on technique could ever teach, and the one thing that comes to us parents, too, as a pure gift.

Do-Overs or No Do-Overs?

When talking about the seculosity of parenting, we cannot overlook what happens on sidelines and in bleachers and backstage.

I'm referring to fathers who cannot restrain themselves from arguing with referees at their kids' sports games and mothers who primp their daughters within an inch of their lives for television auditions and beauty contests. These are cases of parental overinvestment that go beyond merely wanting your child to do their best, or even establish public enoughness. Journalist Katie Roiphe asks,

> I can't help but wonder if all of the effort poured into creating the perfect child is a way of deflecting and rechanneling adult disappointment. Are these parents, so virtuously exhausted, so child-drained at the end of one of these busy days, compensating for something they have given up? Something missing in their marriage? Some romantic disappointment? Some compromise of career or adventure?

Sometimes the dynamic Roiphe describes is explicit, but usually it's hidden. Part of us wants our child to be liked—in a certain way—in grade school because we still remember what it was like not to be picked first at kickball or to hear of kids having sleepovers that we weren't invited to. Never mind that our son doesn't like kickball and our daughter has no idea about the sleepovers in question, those old wounds still hurt. It's not just that we want to spare them that pain, we believe instinctively that their triumph will redress our own failure.

This is parenting as redemption, with the child cast in the role of savior. They cease to be a person in their own right and become our second chance to get into the school that rejected us, follow the dream we didn't have the guts to stick with, enjoy the childhood or adolescence we were denied, or leverage the physical prowess or beauty that we squandered (or never had). What's involved here is nothing short of the objectification of one's progeny.

It may take until their teenage years, possibly their twenties, but children who've been objectified in this way rarely fail to make their feelings known. They may do so with words. They may do so with their wardrobe or who they choose to date. They may do so by moving across the country. As parents, perhaps the best we can do is to pray that the rebellion happens early and with as few felonies as possible.

One final and related way we practice the seculosity of parenting—perhaps the most obvious way—pertains to that dreaded word, *legacy*. A friend told me recently that his first thought when his daughter was born was that now he could die.[18] He meant that whatever the afterlife held for him personally, his genes had now been passed on, and he could breathe easy that his line would not end with him. He and his wife had not only given the world something beautiful with this baby, they had preserved and perpetuated a part of themselves.

Reproduction as a means of immortality—a path to eternal life—brings us squarely into religious territory. As tempting as it may be, the rejoinder to this strategy is embarrassingly plain: think of yourself as the child in the scenario. Even if we love and admire our progenitors, no child wants to be subsumed into a parent's identity. The son who inherits the company his father started doesn't see himself as an extension of the old man but as his successor, maybe his better. If he doesn't, then onlookers will make

---

18. My feeling after the birth of my first child was the exact opposite—in that moment I knew had to take a better care of myself so that these boys weren't denied a father. Time to rein in the burgers.

sure he's aware of all the ways he's not his dad. The daughter who takes over the family's nonprofit may be proud of her roots but has her own contribution to make. Our parenting style will vary from that of our folks as a result not only of cultural shifts but of the gifts and perspective our coparent brings to the table.

Besides, a person only has so much control over their legacy. None of us will be there to dictate the terms. What we want to be remembered for and what we end up being remembered for—*if* we're remembered—are often two separate things. Just ask Pete Rose or Bette Nesmith Graham.[19]

Which is not to suggest that our children aren't a big part of what we leave behind, both the good *and* the bad, merely that thinking of them in those terms tends to convey a pressure that inspires rebellion rather than respect.

Notes from a Dragon Mom

For a less religious approach to raising kids—parenting as child-rearing rather than mom or dad's road to enoughness and immortality—we need look no further than Emily and Ronan Rapp.

Ronan Rapp was born with Tay-Sachs disease, a rare genetic disorder for which there is no treatment and no cure. His mother, Emily, documented his short life in a blog that she turned into a book, *The Still Point of a Turning World*, capturing the heartbreaking

---

19. Nesmith Graham was a typist who hit it big when she invented Liquid Paper, which is what she would have been remembered for if her only son Michael hadn't gone on to fame as one of The Monkees. But examples of people who were unknown in their time and now revered, or vice versa, are endless: author Franz Kafka, painter Elizabeth Thompson, the Bay City Rollers, etc.

yet utterly beautiful experience of parenting a child with a terminal diagnosis.[20]

All the secondary concerns go out the window. It doesn't matter what kind of food you feed the child, or what sleeping method you favor, or how many music classes they take, it will not alter their genetics or extend their life. You still care about some of those decisions, but not as much.

More pressingly, parenting a child with a terminal diagnosis means throwing out whatever plans or expectations you may have had for the child's future. The situation forces a parent to live in the present-tense in the most vivid of ways. Before he died, Emily wrote,

> I have abandoned the future, and with it any visions of Ronan's scoring a perfect SAT or sprinting across a stage with a Harvard diploma in his hand. We're not waiting for Ronan to make us proud. We don't expect future returns on our investment. We've chucked the graphs of developmental milestones and we avoid parenting magazines at the pediatrician's office. Ronan has given us a terrible freedom from expectations, a magical world where there are no goals, no prizes to win, no outcomes to monitor, discuss, compare.

She goes on to describe the day-to-day of parenting in this way as "often peaceful, even blissful." The only task is to love, the only activity to make sure Ronan's brief time is as comfortable and

---

20. Ronan died in February 2013, just before his third birthday.

dignified as can be arranged. Emily calls herself not a tiger mom but a dragon parent: "fierce and loyal and loving as hell."

As moving as her testimony reads, the circumstances may feel too extreme for us to relate. Yet Emily suggests that the lessons she's had to learn apply more widely. Because no one ultimately escapes a terminal diagnosis—no parent and no child.

The terrible freedom she mentions is freedom nonetheless: to love your children as they are and for who they are, rather than who they will be or who you want them to become (and what that will say about you). It is the freedom to cherish their being over their doing, radically so, the actual present over the possible future. Emily invokes a form of love that is fundamentally unconcerned with results or behavior (because it can't be) and is all the more powerful for it. In doing so, she allows us a peek at what uncoerced, unconditional love really looks like in human relationships.

More than that, she gives us a glimpse of grace, the way Christians believe that God loves his children. A "noncontingent, compassionate alliance" is how one of my mentors once phrased it.

In the seculosity of parenting, the threat of judgment looms over the parent's every breath. Enoughness lies in the balance. Grace, on the other hand, begins from the standpoint that nothing that needs to be done hasn't already been done. Enoughness is an irrevocable gift of God, secured by Christ himself. Or as Martin Luther wrote in thesis twenty-six of the Heidelberg Disputation (1518), "the law says 'do this', and it is never done. Grace says, 'believe in this' and everything is already done."

The resultant freedom is far from terrible. It flows from the knowledge that God is in the business of loving short-sighted, overinvested, and overwhelmed parents of all stripes—and that death, to paraphrase Martin Luther King Jr., is a comma, not a period.

Grace bursts the boundaries of our every careful philosophy, pronouncing the freedom to play, to serve, to love, to laugh, to cry, to wait, to work, to be a child, and yes, even to have one.

CHAPTER 4

THE SECULOSITY
OF TECHNOLOGY

t's the early 1890s, and two men in Paris are overheard talking:

> "When the bell rings, you get up and answer it?" one asks.
> "Why, yes. Certainly," his friend replies.
> "I see. Just like a servant," concludes the first man.

The pair in question are renowned artists Edgar Degas and Jean-Louis Forain, and the one overhearing them happens to be their colleague, French impressionist painter Pierre-Auguste Renoir. Under discussion is the technological miracle that had recently set the city abuzz: the telephone. Forain took pride in being one of the first people in the city to own one. Degas, to his credit, could see the writing on the wall. Under the auspices of innovation, Forain had become the servant of that which was designed to serve him. He had willingly—almost proudly—subordinated himself, ready to be summoned at the clang of the bell.

If Degas was skeptical of the power that those early telephones could exert, what a field day he would have had with the "smart" kind.

Anyone who has interrupted a lunch conversation to check a text message knows what Degas was getting at. After hearing that little ding, we come running, hoping perhaps for a little hit of affection or excitement or direction.

Flash to 2016 and I'm approaching the counter at our local cell-phone supplier. The guy manning the desk had clearly seen my kind before: a little on edge, determined to say their piece before losing their nerve, not unlike a high-school kid asking out a prom date. Which was pretty much how I felt—determined yet slightly out of body, desperate to get through with it, and leaning heavily on Cheap Trick to drown out any second thoughts.

The clerk did not demur, thank God. He nodded, took my iPhone into custody, made a couple of entries in his computer, and issued me a brand-new flip phone. All of a sudden, it was 2005 again.

Trigger pulled, I took a breath and asked how many other similar models he had sold this month. "More than you'd think," he replied. It wasn't quite the pat on the back I was hoping for.

I had not come lightly to the decision to abandon my smartphone. The polite explanation involved wanting a bit more mental space. The honest truth was that I didn't have the self-restraint not to check the thing at every stoplight and during every trip to the bathroom. Even watching television had become a two-screen experience. What sealed the deal was when my four-year-old drew pictures of everyone in the family, taking extra care to place a phone in my hand. That felt the opposite of good. To be a servant is one thing, a slave another.

Phone calls and text messages were not the problem. I couldn't handle having the internet in my pocket. Like many of my peers, I had come to rely on the affirmation and distraction it provided on a moment-to-moment basis: affirmation of my enoughness and distraction from my not-enoughness. Seculosity lurked behind every click.

I had informed my wife about the decision months earlier. Even though she'd been gingerly advocating for such a move for a while, she chuckled and said she'd believe it when she saw it. Weeks came and went, and reasons to delay kept presenting themselves. What would I do for directions? And I needed a good camera— you know, for the kids. Oh and what if the website I edit crashed? Better to wait until summer, when traffic subsides.

Rationalizations aside, my only legitimate hesitation had to do with how I would negotiate the smugness that flip phones radiate. Every time a friend or colleague had pulled one out in recent months, whether or not they drew attention to it, everyone in the vicinity fell over themselves to offer excuses about their own smartphone usage or make awkward jokes about being addicted to social media. Among parents of small children, where distraction constitutes a major source of guilt, the mere presence of a flip phone *condemns*—and no one wants to be a lightning rod of judgment.

The way I saw it, the flip phone was an admission of weakness, not a display of strength. Plenty of my peers enjoyed healthy—or health*ier*—relationships with their devices. For them, the smartphone screen functioned as a resource rather than an escape, a tool rather than a shield. I envied these people. I envied their freedom, and I suppose you get to a point where you envy that freedom more than you care about whatever perceived judgments a personal choice might engender.

I Love Technology, I Swear

Like all forms of seculosity, the seculosity of technology isn't really about technology. Nor does it pertain to the internet specifically, inseparable as the two subjects may be at this point. Technology itself is impersonal and amoral. Microchips are not inherently good or evil; innovation simply unfurls—and we adapt to it, not the other way around. We attach values to how these things are used and experienced, not the things themselves.

Besides, when it comes to something like the internet, there are too many upsides to count. I'm thinking of parents video-chatting with toddlers when they're away from home, of micro-philanthropy getting resources to people in need. The democratization of educational and creative opportunities—museums and libraries and cinemas that are just a click away. Conveniences abound where they didn't before. Those who pine for the days of booking air travel over the phone or waiting in line at the bank to check their balance would likely pine for anything, God bless their Muzak-loving hearts.

Personally, I think of the long-distance relationship my wife and I had when we were dating, the jokes that only work over text. I think about the amount of great music I've discovered online, the wonderful sermons I've listened to, the fresh voices I've read, and the discussions I've been privy to. I think of the message boards that have kept track of a relative's progress during chemotherapy.

The benefits of internet technology—the good it makes possible—are obvious. The liabilities are less so. These, we are only beginning to understand.

What's increasingly clear is that, old or young, male or female, black or white, religious or not, the internet is no longer an escape from the everyday so much as an increasingly large part of it. Any account of modern life—spiritual or otherwise—that ignores our relationship to such technology will fall flat.

And yet, writing about technology is a notoriously dicey undertaking, first of all because of the fluidity. What's true today may not be true tomorrow. More than that, go on record with too much disparagement and you risk the accusation of being a Luddite, which is code for old-fashioned, irrelevant, dying. In a culture that values the New, the Now, and the Next, few more shameful labels exist. You might as well call someone a heretic and get it over with.[21]

The stakes are too high, however, to avoid the subject out of fear of insult. And anyhow, the seculosity of technology flourishes among those who appreciate their devices, not those who shun them.

This is not to suggest that everyone who owns a smartphone should trade it in for a flip, only that when you ask people today to locate the source of their stress and exhaustion, they will more often than not mention the unsustainable pace of life that smart technology has mandated. With everything at our fingertips, all the time, the rule of the playground reigns: you snooze, you lose—forever and ever, amen.

A friend recently described the internet as "just like the real world, but with all the forgiveness vacuumed out." What he meant was that the web, by its very nature, privileges economy over precision, telling over showing, and yelling over telling. Opinions must

---

21. Age today has undoubtably taken on an inverted moral dimension from our ancestors' conception. Young is good, and old is, well, not as good. Get with the program or be left in the dust. Whatever you do, don't be a hater.

be pronounced as quickly and stridently as possible if they are to register on our personal scoreboard. As James Hamblin puts it, "the Internet launders outrage and returns it to us as validation, in the form of likes and stars and hearts. The greatest return comes from a strong and superior point of view, on high moral ground."

In other words, all those zeroes and ones have created a place where our striving after righteousness can operate independent of bodily limitations like, you know, the need for sleep. The ensuing anxiety, loneliness, and social breakdown are simply the fruit of self-justification unmoored from flesh and blood.

Seculosity comes into play when technology ceases to be a vehicle for chasing enoughness and becomes the actual source of it. Among the many ways we harness technology as a "guilt management system," the four most popular fall under the headings of optimization, information, distraction, and affirmation.

Optimization Nation

I don't remember hearing the word *optimize* outside of technological circles before 2013. You would optimize the hard drive on your computer, or the transmission of your car, or possibly the space in your closet.

Now we optimize our time, our finances, our bodies, even our relationships. We turn to *lifehacks* to make our lives run more smoothly and ensure we're not wasting any time or energy. We even optimize our church services.[22]

---

22. In a relevant article on the so-called virtue of efficiency in the church, theologian R. Scott Clark laments the rise in Protestant churches of following an intinction-only policy during the celebration of communion—that is, a policy of dipping the wafers into the cup of wine rather than having people

It is no accident that the lexicon of efficiency has worked its way into everyday jargon. Language reflects our priorities, conscious and otherwise, in this case a view of human beings as advanced machines. Thus, we talk casually about how we are "wired" and liken the brain to a computer, our bodies to hardware, and our personalities to software. But as useful as these metaphors may sometimes be, the brain isn't a computer, nor do our limbs contain any metal. The spirit, to say nothing of the soul, is not actually code.

Once we've conceptualized ourselves as glorified androids, we naturally devote our energy to upgrading the system, theoretically even perfecting it. There's no problem that cannot be solved by technology, Silicon Valley's doctrine of technosolutionism tells us. Spend enough time at a tech convention (or watching the HBO show *Silicon Valley*), and you'll hear that language everywhere. Technology companies aren't producing products, they are "making the world a better place" via middle-out compression. Technosolutionism explains why Mark Zuckerberg can preach a gospel of Facebook advancing humanity (the key to preventing pandemics and ending terrorism) even as it frays our social fabric on almost every conceivable level.

The most extreme form of technosolutionism goes by the name transhumanism, and it is there that the religious ramifications are no longer hidden but celebrated. Julian Huxley, a British eugenicist (!) who helped shape the movement into its current form, once defined transhumanism as the "idea of humanity attempting to overcome its limitations and to arrive at fuller fruition." More

---

drink directly. Pastors publicly reference hygiene as the principal concern behind the move, while privately mentioning time as the main motivation. Intinction is much *quicker* than everyone actually taking the cup.

recent enthusiasts of transhumanism like Ray Kurzweil maintain that, thanks to technology, people "will become posthuman: immortal, limitless, changed beyond recognition," likely by the year 2045. This is technology as salvation, and I highly doubt that its appeal and influence will wane in coming years.

In an essay on the religiosity of transhumanism, writer Meghan O'Gieblyn observes that, despite their oft-voiced disdain for conventional religion, transhumanists "tend to sound an awful lot like early church fathers." She goes on:

> "Uploading does not aim to leave the flesh behind," [digitalist philosopher Eric Steinhart] writes; "on the contrary, it aims *at the intensification of the flesh.*" The irony is that transhumanists are arguing these questions as though they were the first to consider them. Their discussions give no indication that these debates belong to a theological tradition that stretches back to the earliest centuries of the Common Era.

Believe it or not, the word *transhuman* first appeared in Henry Francis Carey's 1814 translation of Dante's *Paradiso*, the final book of the *Divine Comedy*. Its debut comes after Dante has completed his journey through Paradise and is ascending into heaven. His flesh is transformed, but his new body leaves the poet uncharacteristically speechless. "Words may not tell of that *transhuman* change." There you have it.

The Information Age

Technosolutionism and transhumanism may be the most overt expressions of the seculosity of technology, but they are by no means the most pernicious. Take our relationship with information itself, which has taken on a burdensome aspect in recent years. Data is *everywhere*. Back in 2013 some brave individual broke the news that 90 percent of the world's electronic data was created in just the past two years. Today, I'd be surprised if the number wasn't closer to 95 percent.

When I say data is everywhere, I'm not only referring to the user data we generate every time we log on to the internet. I'm talking about the Communion rail. Spend much time behind it, and you'll become an expert on wristwear. (This feels almost improper to mention. Communion is supposed to be a holy time, with eyes, ears, taste buds, and kneecaps all focused on matters eternal—not on fashion, that most temporal of subjects. Oh well.) As you might expect, you don't see nearly as many watches as you used to. What few you do see tend to be pretty cool; wearing a timepiece has clearly become a statement in recent years. That's not all. Bangles are in, LiveStrong bracelets are out. No surprise there.

By far the biggest trend I've witnessed in my decade of semi-professional chalice-ing is the fitness tracker. If I had to estimate, I'd say one-in-eight people taking Communion at our church currently sports some variation of the device. Ten years ago they were nonexistent. A fitness tracker is a slim, colorful band that takes a person's pulse and records her movements. It tells its wearer how many steps they've taken in a day, the distance traveled, the calories burned. It can monitor sleep and give you a printout of your REM cycles. The most popular brand at the moment goes by the name Fitbit, but Apple Watches serve basically the same purpose. Fitbit once marketed their product as something that will help its buyer "stay motivated, reach goals and find your fit. Because fitness doesn't follow a formula. It's the sum of your life." Wowza.

On their own, fitness trackers are straightforward. The information they provide can be heeded or ignored; it can help a person or not, depending on how it is used or interpreted. Considered as a larger trend, though, the boom in fitness trackers represents a step forward in the mission to leave no corner of daily experience unquantified. I'm not sure who decided that everything we do must be counted, tallied, collated, but I do know that if an activity isn't documented, it may as well have not happened.

Alas, where there is data, there is measurement. Even the most mundane task can, when quantified, become a point of comparison. That's the allure of all this previously unknown information—to chart ourselves (and others) to find out how we're doing, whether we are improving or getting worse—whether we are, in the final tally, enough.

Some companies have begun issuing fitness trackers to their employees. The formal line is that they're promoting wellness, but efficiency undoubtedly plays a role. Filling the position and training the replacement of a worker who's been laid low by a heart attack doesn't do wonders for the bottom line, after all.

One way these trackers are being put to use is via corporate fitness challenges, with incentives going to those whose score best. Needless to say, as with all public scorekeeping endeavors, the pressure to assert our enoughness inspires more than just hard work. The *Wall Street Journal* reported on a friendly contest among sales executives in Utah to see who could take the most steps in a week. With five hours to go, Dan Adams was trailing. "So Mr. Adams taped his Fitbit activity tracker to the blade of an electric saw and left it vibrating on a work bench. When he returned early the next morning, the saw's vibrations had registered 57,000 steps."

The Acronym That Is Destroying My Soul

Fitness trackers are just one expression of the seculosity of Big Data, and a fairly innocuous one at that. What about your inbox or feed? "Staying on top of things" is another increasingly treasured form of righteousness. More and more of us compete over being well informed and feel guilty about falling behind.

For some, the attempt to manage the flood of information coming across our screens—from news stories to pop culture to personal sharing—has turned frantic, even desperate. Unfortunately, as anyone who has spent vacation days cleaning up their old emails or delving into their backlog of social media can corroborate, the mountaintop never quite arrives.

Again, on the surface, this appears to be a rather asinine problem. Yet aspiring to be *caught up* is not a neutral drive, not when *caught up* encompasses a limitless set of info. The very attempt keeps us squarely focused on ourselves, breeding first competition, then antagonism, and, ultimately, despondency.

Journalist Elizabeth Minkel hinted at the risks in what she referred to as "the online acronym that is destroying my soul," ICYMI. Those five letters often precede social media posts or forwards of must-read articles. It stands for In Case You Missed It, and the implied mentality goes something like this:

> ICYMI makes staying connected feel like a constant game of catch-up. . . . ICYMI is a tacit acknowledgement of that psychological finish line, always being moved an inch more out of reach—I can feel it now, chipping away at me.

The problem is not information on its own but the accompanying imperative about staying abreast of it all, which is fed, presumably, by the need to master, to prove our relevance, to justify our existence. Technology has just made the pursuit more convenient. Minkel's words evoke those of Saint Paul, who described life held captive to the Law as "a curse" (Galatians 3:10).

Ironically, the pace at which we process information tends to have an adverse effect on the information itself (to say nothing of our blood pressure), placing true mastery that much more out of reach. That is, in order to stand out amid the melee of output—to achieve recognition and thereby affirmation—writers both amateur and professional are forced to reduce or sensationalize their messages, emphasizing the aspects that will get the most immediate response and leaving out those that might encumber its accessibility. When clicks equal revenue, the triumph of sloganeering and "fake news" is a foregone conclusion.

One of the great coups of the seculosity of technology has been to encourage users to think of our online presences more and more in terms of personal branding. The faster you respond to a given event online, and the bolder the terms you use—be it a friend's engagement or a political election—the higher the chance that someone will read it, and your brand will grow. You are justified not by what you say so much as *that* you say it. So the louder the better, especially if what you have to say is scornful. That the internet rewards not just brevity but outrage may not exactly be earth-shattering news, I know.

Something deeply cultish flowers here. The better you get at managing your messages—the closer you get to the elusive #InboxZero—the more emails that arrive in your inbox. "Just when I thought I was out," you can almost hear Al Pacino complain, "they pull me back in."

Historical parallels for this phenomenon abound. Toward the end of the nineteenth century, "labor-saving" devices promised to transform the lives of housewives and domestic servants across Europe and North America. Thanks to technological innovations like the vacuum cleaner, a carpet could be spotless in a matter of minutes. Washing machines made time-consuming contraptions like the mangle obsolete.

Yet, as the historian Ruth Schwartz Cowan demonstrates in her 1983 book *More Work for Mother*, the result was not an increase in leisure time among those charged with doing the housework. Instead, as the efficiency of housework increased, so did the standards of cleanliness and domestic order we came to expect. Now that the hallway carpet could be kept spotless, it had to be; now that fraying sleeves could be easily mended, they were all but outlawed.

In a similar way, now that we *can* respond to work emails in bed at midnight, we are expected to. As righteousness escalates, so does burnout.

The Attraction of Distraction

Since everyone pretty much acknowledges the crazy-making qualities of smart technology, its hooks must run deep for us to continue to use it to such an extent. As the transhumanist movement makes clear, the appeal boils down to control, not just over death but life. We rely on technology to aid us in the quest for enoughness. The strategy is twofold and—you guessed it—eerily religious: first, to abate condemnation and second, to pronounce absolution.

Thinkers as diverse as Nietzsche, Pascal, and Louis C.K. have understood our preoccupation with stimulation as evidence of a fear of silence. Stimulation, regardless of how trivial or pixelated, distracts us from that which we would rather not feel. It anesthetizes.

Again, our attraction to distraction predates Apple by a long shot. It goes back to what Steve Jobs's iconic logo references: the ur-Apple of Eden (and its missing bite). We have always sought to distract ourselves from pain and guilt; what's changed is the ease with which we can now do so.

David Foster Wallace articulated this theory in his unfinished novel *The Pale King*:

> Maybe dullness is associated with psychic pain because something that's dull or opaque fails to provide enough stimulation to distract people from some other, deeper type of pain that is always there, if only in an ambient low-level way, and which most of us spend nearly all our time and energy trying to distract ourselves from feeling, or at least feeling directly or with our full attention.

In other words, we flee from boredom because of what we encounter there, namely, ourselves. Wallace's theory extends just as much to the production of information as the consumption of it, the output just as much as the input. Screens distract us from our core pain, which is the pain of not being enough, the reality of our finitude, what some call existential angst.

A theologian might ascribe these impulses to the avoidance of a *different* sort of information: the verdict of God's Law—that we are found guilty, terminally so. It's ironic, then, that we often respond to modern distractibility by moralizing it, shaming parents and teenagers into paying better attention lest they face public disapproval. Since we are often distracting ourselves from some sense of condemnation in the first place, the dynamic feeds on itself.

Yet there's another element at work. In addition to distracting us from unpleasantness, technology provides users with the illusion of autonomy. When we're sitting at a stoplight and reach to check our email, we achieve momentary liberation from restrictive circumstances. We use our phone to shake the bars of a temporary prison cell, to push back "against the indignity of being made to wait."

Put another way, we use technology to rebel against anything that would seek to constrain or confine us. To the Law that tells us we are creatures, men and women with limits and dependencies, we shake our fists and insist we are Creators. I can handle things just fine on my own—especially if the car behind me would stop honking and let me think straight for a second.

I kid, but the fact remains that there is nothing less autonomous than a gaggle of people glued to their smartphones. This is the cruel irony to which Degas alluded so deftly: our addiction to control ends up controlling us.

To the degree that distraction fuels the seculosity of technology, it also displaces genuine religiosity. One of the refrains I hear most often from those who attend the church where I work has to do with how much they enjoy the silence. What they mean is that there are fewer and fewer spaces left where passivity can reliably be experienced, where just sitting there is not frowned upon but understood as laudatory, even necessary—and they crave it. They may not be able to quote any of the creeds or tell me what the sermon meant, but they know refuge when they experience it.

In a culture of distraction, the pauses built into the liturgy of a church service can be downright subversive. They point to an alternate mode of life—of human *being* rather than human *doing*, as the cliché goes—a sacred order marked by calm rather than effort. Essayist Andrew Sullivan believes that "the reason we live in a culture increasingly without faith is not because science has somehow disproved the unprovable, but because the white noise of secularism has removed the very stillness in which it might endure or be reborn."

I agree wholeheartedly, which is why it makes me sad when religious leaders try to entice people into the pews by means of fresh, religiously sanitized distractions, or when they see it as their "missional duty" to craft services in which each and every moment is filled with language or light. It's not an accident that large numbers of young people who grew up in flashy Evangelical churches have ended up Greek Orthodox. You can't blame them.

Yet let us not fool ourselves into believing that silence and stillness on their own are enough. We have every reason to fear those things, were it not for the God we encounter there, the "Mediator and Advocate" who suffered divine silence, once for all. But I'm getting ahead of myself.

Affirmation Station

While the seculosity of technology thrives in part because of how handily it abates condemnation, the ultimate reason we are willing to indenture ourselves to the ring of the bell has to do with love. When that little ding goes off, we hear the allure of affirmation. We've already explored how this plays out on social media, the identities we project and pine after.

But the promise goes deeper. Whatever your conviction or interest, no matter how fringe or toxic, a community exists online that will reinforce it. A few clicks are all it takes to find allies who will confirm the righteousness of your opinions, as well as common enemies to fortify your tribe. It's intoxicating, radicalizing, and more often than not dehumanizing.

Occasionally the physical remove proves beneficial. For those who have been burned in some fashion, for example, the web can engender safety to engage with someone or something we otherwise find threatening. Finding others who have undergone specific traumas or tragedies—or simply like the same canceled TV show as us—does allow a person to feel less alone. But it is nigh on impossible to deny that, divorced from body language and nonverbal cues, we are less likely to internalize affirmation when it does come our way and much more likely to objectify and demonize those with whom we disagree.

No wonder the internet has not ushered in a new age of mutual understanding on hot-button issues but instead deepened the divides.[23] If given just one word to describe a tool designed to promote communication—and to a lesser extent, global harmony—that turned out to hinder it, some might go with *ironic*. I'd choose *biblical*.

Indeed, a decade of daily blogging has taught me that people, myself included, often live off the ideas we disagree with in a strangely parasitic way. A rush ensues when we perceive a threat, and our self-justification muscles spring into overdrive. How else do you explain the phenomenon of hate-reading/-watching? Whether the topic is breastfeeding or drone warfare or Christian theology,

---

23. Nowhere is this more pronounced than in the discussion of Religion.

the same dynamics are at play. Our brains sense a challenge and switch into combat mode, activating a rhetorical merry-go-round.

In fact, several studies of online behavior suggest that the angrier we get on a particular subject, the less likely we are to be right about it. Meaning, if we have a clear enemy in our minds against whom we define ourselves and our arguments, then our own views are probably not as trustworthy as we think they are. They are being dictated not by truth but by our own drive for justification vis-à-vis our opponent. Oftentimes what passes for debate online is actually a form of peripheral signaling to like-minded individuals, who we hope will give us the acceptance we so long for.

Perhaps this is where cynicism ends and compassion takes over, when we realize that the digital wind howls a tune that is neither new nor particularly informative. It is one we all know: acknowledge me, affirm me, love me, tell me I'm enough. This is the age-old cry of the human heart, a cacophony not of fact or opinion but of need, a glimpse of what God must hear when listening to his children—to you and to me.

If that's the case, then there's hope—real hope—for those stuck in the seculosity of technology. But it doesn't take the form of a flip phone.

Backflipping

You see, nine months after switching to a flip phone, I went back to a smart one. What got me in the end wasn't the web itself, but music and texts. They were the rationalization, in any case.

I realized about a month into the experiment that I wasn't willing to live in a world where music wasn't mobile. Walkmans and Discmans were faithful companions long before cell phones entered the picture; I can't (and don't want to) imagine traveling without a soundtrack. The last straw was when the CD player in my car broke, leaving the auxiliary cable my only option for tunes. It was as though the Lord himself had granted me plausible deniability. Thus, like a bad illustration of Romans 7, I started carrying around my decommissioned iPhone in the pocket not occupied by my flip phone. It looked as ridiculous as it sounds, a fact that my colleagues and loved ones wasted no time in bringing to my attention.

Texts were the other reason. Call me naïve, but I hadn't realized how much I—and everyone in my vicinity—had come to rely on text messaging to communicate. The flip phone could accomplish a basic message, sure, and the extra taps weren't the end of the world. They usually made people laugh. Still, pretty much all nonessential texting was eliminated, and what texting I did do became extraordinarily economical. This wouldn't have been a problem even two years beforehand. But now it gave off the impression of impatience and even rudeness. People would ask me if I was okay, if I was upset about something, why I hadn't responded to their message ("Because I was about to *see* you," I'd huffily reply). I found myself making excuses for my less-than-effervescent text etiquette—not exactly the most endearing position when you've just met someone.

Basically, my relationships began to suffer. Like a vegan on the Fourth of July, I was the guy you had to plan around (the only difference being that people today tend to be pretty accommodating of dietary restrictions). But that address or picture you're trying to send me? Would you mind emailing it instead? Oh and forget about communicating with anyone under twenty-five. In short, my issue became everyone else's. It wasn't just car stereos that had moved on.

The hope for those stuck in the seculosity of technology isn't hope that turns a blind eye to those things that make the internet such a desolate landscape. It is one that accounts for and addresses them. It is hope in the reality of a God who does not abandon his creatures to their compulsions, prideful or otherwise. A God who we are told *gave up* control for the sake of an embittered, exhausted world—who did not come to be served but to serve, and to make a definitive break with the endless cycle of condemnation and justification.

This God, I have found, is not put off by our stubborn attempts to secure on our own steam what is given freely, but through forgiveness grants people like me the assurance and therefore safety to experience their pain head-on. The implications are no less immediate than the technologies that seek to subvert them. According to theologian Ted Peters:

> Once we realize that we can get out of the business of justifying ourselves, the world suddenly looks different. No longer do we need to defend ourselves from a hostile world by identifying ourselves with what is good or just or true. We can live in the world—we can love the world—as if it is our world, with or without the lines we draw between good and evil.

Perhaps this is the peace of mind evinced by Mary, who sat enrapt at Christ's feet while her distracted sister Martha kept score and pleaded for Christ to do the same (Luke 10:38–42). He refused then, and he refuses now. Martha did not need technology to turn her into an exhausted, self-justifying wreck. Yet her failure to

surrender control did not disqualify her for the "one thing need-
ful," thank God. It formed the doorway through which Christ
reached out to her.

Who knows, to the extent that distraction is killing us (and
we are too distracted to notice), it may be bringing us into contact with the divine in a way that no amount of carefully chosen,
quietly contemplated words can. Because the God who dwells in
silence does not exist independent of the noise, nor is he waiting
for you and me to calm our own storms. Miraculous as it may
sound, I've heard he even has a predilection for hopeless rational-
izers and their hypocritical friends.

I read it online so it has to be true.

CHAPTER 5

THE SECULOSITY
OF WORK

True story: in 1965, Congress held a lengthy hearing to discuss the looming twenty-hour work week. According to their estimates, the rapidly expanding automation of the day meant that by the year 2000, Americans would have more free time than they'd know what to do with. Summer camps would have to stay open year-round. People would be taking so many vacation trips that our national infrastructure would need to be completely overhauled to accommodate the traffic.[24]

Talk about an astonishing lack of insight! Technological advances have not increased downtime. Instead of condensing work, they have squeezed out rest. Dramatically so.

---

24. To be fair, Congress wasn't acting completely without precedent. In 1930, pioneering economist John Maynard Keynes wrote an essay titled "Economic Possibilities for Our Grandchildren" in which he estimated that by the time his grandchildren had grown up, roughly today, people would be working just fifteen hours a week.

A cartoon strip that went viral a few years ago captured the wider reality. The image shows a man and woman lying on a sunny beach, listening to the waves. The woman reads a book while the man types on his laptop. The caption reads: "I'm not a workaholic. I just work to relax."

The punchline hits too close to home for comfort. The number of arguments my wife and I have gotten into over my inability to stop working after hours or on vacation—like sneaking into the bathroom to answer an email—let's just say it isn't pretty. "The internet doesn't take a break," I protest, by way of justification. "You're *not* the internet," she tells me. I do a little robot dance to try to defuse the situation, but we both know I don't deserve her.

Alas, I'm not alone. Despite boasting the smallest amount of paid days off, the United States leads the developed world in untaken vacation days. We clock in some 1,788 hours a year, 120 more than our counterparts in Britain, 300 more than the French, and 400 more than the Germans.

We may *think* we want to "get away from it all," we may complain about the nonstop pace of today's economy, but these numbers tell a different story. People who for the most part have the means and opportunity to take a week or two off every year opt not to. The only conclusion a person can draw is that many of us who claim to want some R&R are either fibbing or in the grip of something stronger than ourselves.

The real question when it comes to our work habits is not so much why we work such insane hours, but why we have come to *prefer* it. Could it be that our careers provide us with much more than a paycheck? Welcome to what may be our single most enthralling replacement religion, the seculosity of work.

Sure, increased hours at the office could have something to do with the fact that work has become that much more enjoyable an experience, that in contrast to previous generations, drudgery has diminished. American prosperity allows more and more people to seek work according to interest and convenience, rather than necessity or parental decree. As a result, part of the attraction to overwork could be the passion and curiosity that more and more people bring to their careers.

At the very least, the office no longer represents a necessary-if-tiring diversion from the main stuff of life so much as a central element of it. Popular sitcoms like *The Office*, *Parks and Recreation*, and *30 Rock* mimic this cultural shift of gravity by setting their shows in the workplace rather than the home, as was the common practice in the 1980s and '90s (*Family Ties*, *Facts of Life*, *Roseanne*). That, or the home has *become* the workplace, as in *Keeping Up with the Kardashians*. Every waking moment now contributes to the brand.

Companies like Google and Pixar have picked up on these more amenable attitudes toward work and run with them, designing their offices to resemble playgrounds, complete with ping-pong tables, fancy snacks, and state-of-the-art video games. Other companies like Netflix have introduced flex-day policies that permit employees to take as much vacation as they want—as long as they complete their work.

Where some see perks, others see a ploy to blur work into life and life into work. A friend at a local tech firm relayed the story of touring his company's new headquarters with some younger colleagues. The most pressing question they had for their boss was whether or not they would be able to bring their pets to work. Such a question would have never occurred to their parents. But it's not (necessarily) because they're being coddled. *The Onion* memorably lampooned the underlying ethos with their headline, "Laid-Back Company Allows Employees to Work from Home after 6PM." As one of Amazon's running office jokes goes, "work-life balance is for people who do not like their work." Ha ha . . . *ha?*

When we live to work rather than the other way around, the distinction between our jobs and our selves understandably disappears. In the Bible, Saint Paul often takes issue with those who depend on "good works" for their righteousness. Today we've simply subtracted the "good" part.

The seculosity of work may have reached absurd heights but that doesn't mean it's a laughing matter. A clinical social worker in the Bay Area who sees a number of patients in the tech and start-up sector explained the mentality of her patients this way: "Everyone wants to be a model employee. . . . One woman told me: 'The expectation is not that you should work smart, it's that you should work hard. It's just do, do, do, until you can't do anymore.'"

Sadly, the stakes run higher than merely fatigue or burn-out. That same interview goes on to detail the suicide of Joseph Thomas, a software engineer at Uber. Speaking to the media afterward, Thomas's widow made no bones about blaming the unapologetic workaholism perpetuated by her husband's company.

A Wonderful Refuge?

If you are someone fortunate enough to enjoy what you do from nine to five, you likely consider it a privilege not to be taken for granted. After all, the idea that we would find our work personally fulfilling is a radical one, historically speaking. Enjoyment, however, constitutes only a partial if not superficial answer to the question of American workaholism.

A less flattering theory for why we prefer the desk to the couch might be that, like technology, our work distracts us from deeper, less manageable realities. Raising children, for example, is a complicated, confusing process, where what you put in as a parent does not always correlate to what you get out. Not so with work. As columnist Ryan Avent observes, "the eclipsing of life's other complications is part of the reward [of workaholism]. It is a cognitive and emotional relief to immerse oneself in something all-consuming while other difficulties float by. The complexities of intellectual puzzles are nothing to those of emotional ones. Work is a wonderful refuge."

To phrase this theory in religious terminology, if work has traditionally been a means of appeasing judgment, today it is that *and* a way of fleeing from it, simultaneously. Constant grinding makes a perfect diversion from conscience or loneliness or grief or vulnerability—a way of imposing order on the chaos of relating to another person or oneself. We find security and even comfort in a head-down mentality, no matter how illusory our destination or finish line may be. In this way, addictive behavior in relation to work makes sense. Just try telling a workaholic that she needs to cut back her hours and see what happens.

And yet, the ultimate reason we work so hard has to do with a harder truth: work has always served as the great American barometer of worth and identity. Our occupation is the number one socially approved means of justifying our existence, and not just the type of occupation but our performance there. When we talk about success or failure in life, it's *assumed* that we're talking about work, which means that a job is never just a job but an identity. It is where we locate our enoughness, and as such, the spring from which our strictest pieties flow.

I remember speaking to a man who had experienced enough success in his career to retire early. After a scare related to his heart, he decided to buy a little farm in rural North Carolina and devote himself full-time to cultivating that land. After a month or so on the farm, though, he came up with an excuse to go back to work—despite the fierce protestations of his splintering family and exasperated doctor. He spoke about not wanting to be put out to pasture, as though productivity and vitality were the same thing. For him, as for many others, a conflation of the two is reflexive.

I do not mean to suggest that work isn't a part of who we are; of course it is. But this man had become synonymous with his occupation, causing everyone around him quite a bit of pain, himself most of all. Sitting still was simply not an option. He needed to *produce*, both to know he was alive and to forget he was going to die.

Another friend accepted a promotion recently on the condition that she take a mandatory six-week break before beginning the new position. What I thought would be a relief turned out to be anything but. She told me she was afraid of stepping off the treadmill, worried about falling behind her peers. She could not accept the reward for which she had (theoretically) been working. The fear of coming up short, of failure—of what religious people might call condemnation—had infected her every waking moment in a way that would make a Puritan blush.

Gesundheit—Not!

This same dynamic informs our relationship to sick days. America, notoriously, does not require employers to offer paid sick leave. On average, employers granted new employees just eight sick days in 2016, down 20 percent since 1993. And even then, people seldom take their sick days when they should.

Recreational complaining about sick colleagues who come into work instead of staying at home has become a mainstay of American flu season. Journalist Daniel Engber put his finger on the issue when he identified the coworker "who comes in to work, red-eyed and drippy, and puts his germy fingers on the handle of the coffeepot or the button of the microwave door. He could have called in sick, but that would take a modicum of decency. No, this guy is a 'team player.' He's a cubicle Cal Ripken Jr., the office iron man with Sudafed." Every office has one, I'm told.

Contracting something from a coworker, since it so rarely happens, serves as a smokescreen for our real concern.[25] The deeper pathology has to do with a presenteeism that implies "if you're not overworked—or won't go into the office sick—you're a slouch." There exists an unspoken competition for extra credit in the boss's eye, where one person slowing down entails another getting ahead.

I suspect that we would be far less worried about our coworkers' health if their presence didn't raise the bar for our own, once the bug from preschool comes home with our toddler. Before you know it, everyone is expected to come in when they're under the weather, for fear of appearing less committed. Unconsciously or not, we treat illness as a threat to corporate efficiency rather than a cause of human suffering.

---

25. You don't need a degree in epidemiology to be familiar with the well-attested truth that we are far more likely to get sick from our kids, public transportation, or our doctor's office than at our place of employment.

When work becomes the primary arbiter of identity, purpose, worth, and community in our lives, it has ceased to function as employment and begun to function as a religion. Or at least we have made it responsible for providing the very things to which we used to look to God.

Procrastinators Unite (Tomorrow)

Perhaps you don't have a full-time job. Or if you do, no one could accuse you of being a workaholic. If you're compulsive about anything, it's procrastination. Certainly *you* are exempt from the seculosity of work, right? Maybe, but maybe not.

In 2010, the American Psychological Association publicized a study reporting that 20 percent of Americans could be qualified as "chronic procrastinators"—a larger percentage than those who suffer from clinical depression (about 7 percent). A separate study a few years earlier made plain what anyone who struggles with the issue knows all too well: the emotion consistently experienced at the time of procrastination, indeed the emotion that defines it as such, is guilt.

Procrastination, then, consists of more than delayed activity but of delayed activity that induces guilt. This means that 20 percent of Americans feel acute guilt over not "getting things done" in a timely matter or not working efficiently enough. Would 20 percent of Americans admit to feeling acute guilt about more conventional moral failures, such as lying or cheating? Doubtful.

If these studies are to be trusted, then it would appear that productivity has surpassed goodness as our society's highest value, our cultural righteousness linked more closely to efficiency than morality. Maybe it always has been.

This makes sense. To procrastinate is to transgress the most precious of capitalist pieties. Dawdling breaks a law that has become, for all intents and purposes, holy: Thou Shalt Produce.

Some say that, despite our bootstrapping past, America has only recently swallowed the whole loaf when it comes to productivity. The *New York Times* theorized:

> Procrastination as epidemic—and the constant guilt that goes with it—is peculiar to the modern era. The 21st-century capitalist world, in its never-ending drive for expansion, consecrates an always-on productivity for the sake of the greater fiscal health.

Epidemic is their word, not mine, but a less hyperbolic one than it might initially seem, in light of what they identify as the real motivating factor. The paper interprets rising procrastination as a byproduct of the "always-on productivity" that a consumerist society "consecrates," or makes sacred. How telling that they cannot avoid religious jargon in their diagnosis.

The Secret to Success Is...Failure?

When it comes to enoughness, productivity and performancism often work in tandem. Rarely do you find one without the other. You could say that the cult of productivity worships the god of success, and you wouldn't be wrong.

Much of productivity's appeal derives from its quantifiability: the more you produce, the more you have, the greater your success, and so forth. In this framework, for something to be worth doing, it must first yield a measurable result. But if you want to climb the extra rung on the ladder, it must yield a measurably *good* result. That might lead a person to avoid those things in which they are not guaranteed success, and never to try anything new.[26]

Not surprisingly, the difference between what constitutes a successful life and a good one often seems perilously thin.

This fixation on success occupies an expanding amount of everyday real estate. Take, for instance, failure. One of the shrewdest triumphs achieved by the cult of productivity has to be the fetishization of failure in evidence over the past decade or so. Whether it be young parents detailing their shortcomings on the internet in the name of "keeping it real," young entrepreneurs mis-appropriating Irish playwright Samuel Beckett's injunction to "fail better" (while attending FailCon!), or best-selling pastors writing books about "failing forward," failure has never enjoyed as positive a profile as it does today.

Something gracious lies behind these misappropriations. Those who feel the freedom to fail tend to take bigger risks and pursue more innovative solutions to problems. I am reminded of a Christian understanding of service, where those whose posi-tion before God has been secured—their acceptance premised on the work of Christ rather than their own—are free to love their neighbors recklessly, even at a cost to themselves. People who have nothing to lose are free to give away everything.

This should not be confused with the "freedom to fail" that many managers preach but that exists in name only. The Chris-tian may never become Mother Teresa, they may prove an utter

---

26. See also: the college admissions process.

failure at good works, but their good standing with God will not be revoked. On the other hand, an employee whose efforts never produce a marketable outcome will eventually be fired—or the company will go out of business.

The careerist endorsement of failure sounds liberating until you realize that no one is actually being let off the hook for their deficiencies. We are instead annexing those shortcomings for the sake of our self-justification, tolerating and in some cases advocating for failure because of its potential fruit, namely, success. We are talking, in other words, about failure only insofar as it serves greater ultimate productivity.

The notion that failure is not failure but the first step toward its opposite may be absurd, but it is also suitably and undeniably cult-like. Ironically, such silver-lining-itis buffers us from the very suffering we are theoretically venerating.

Honest failure, on the other hand, hurts. It is painful. It is out of our control. And there's nothing we like less than that.

Obviously some failures do lead to success. Some dead-ends do herald new beginnings. This is especially true in relationships. But some do not. A biblical truism captures this dynamic: you cannot pole-vault over Good Friday to get to Easter. A death must truly be a death before there can be new life. Christ was not hanging from the cross checking his watch—"another few hours of this and then it's smooth sailing." He really suffered and really died. He experienced true separation from God. What happened thereafter was unexpected.

Which is to say, failure in the service of success is not actually failure.

In Praise of Blizzards

Still not convinced? Perhaps a different tack will help. Perhaps we need to talk about snow days. For all they cover up, snowstorms also expose a number of our less-than-fluffy pieties.

My own childhood snow days are cloaked in soft-focused wonder: a break from routine and school, a time to sled and build forts and drink hot chocolate. I think of Calvin and Hobbes, or Riley's Minnesota memories in Pixar's *Inside Out*.

They bear little resemblance to the snow days of adulthood. There is still beauty to behold and fun to be had, walks to be taken, new recipes to be attempted. But the good parts dissipate far more quickly, especially if you have small children.

In a hurricane or tornado, fear tends to take center stage. The potential for physical damage justifies the attention we divert from other areas of life, pardoning the inconvenience. In a snowstorm, however, once you've made it indoors, safety is rarely a factor.[27] Snowflakes mainly represent an affront to our sense of control, a disruption of plans, unpleasant to the extent those plans have become enshrined. As such, they shine an uncomfortable light on our fragile enoughness.

Writer David Dudley puts it this way: "The snow cares not for your deadlines, your happy hour plans, your scheduled C-section. It wants only to fall on the ground and lie there. And it wants you to, too."

On the flipside, I've been struck by how often the word *freedom* gets mentioned in conjunction with catastrophic weather.

---

27. Unless you live in Siberia or upstate New York.

Freedom from what exactly is unclear, but presumably some sort of accusation related to our to-do list.

Make no mistake: the freedom to reconceive a day according to instinct and opportunity rather than obligation feels pretty good. Because in a proper blizzard, no one is getting any work done—which means that no one is going to overtake us in whatever race we're running. They are snowed in, too. A blizzard is one of a small handful of circumstances that can absolve a person who's trying to justify themselves by their occupation—that can melt the guilt of idleness (pun intended).

At least it should be. As technology has changed how we work, more and more of us refuse to accept the meteorological permission to relax. Instead, we scoff at the very thing that, more often than not, we've been vocally pining for. As long as we have an internet connection, the wheels can keep turning. And even when the power lines go down, every neighborhood contains that one retiree who *has* to shovel his driveway every five seconds, that one young lady who can't *not* get her run in, opting instead to go full-Rocky, regardless of how ridiculous or dangerous it looks.

If the voice from the heavens has shouted STOP, but we can't, no doubt it's because the actual voice we're heeding is that of our real boss, the slave-driver within. The true target of our religiosity comes into focus.

In such instances, it could be that we're dealing not so much with an addiction to productivity or performancism as a fear of sitting still. Anything but silence, our souls and bodies cry out. Alas, not even our devices can fully restore our sense of frantic autonomy. Social media feeds slow to a crawl during a blizzard.

There are only so many fireside snaps or accumulation time-lapses a person can tolerate.

Yet, maybe that's why the blizzard remains the best natural disaster of all, spiritually speaking. The snow falls everywhere, irrespective of our plans and designs, yet remains stunningly personal, burrowing into our eyes and hair and nostrils. It puts our attempts to assert ourselves in perspective. To those who like sledding, the storm ushers in an occasion for joy—and to those who are tired or guilt-ridden, it brings rest.

That's not all. Anyone who has taken a walk or a drive on the day after a massive snowfall will notice how sixteen inches of blanketing looks most beautiful in the places we know to be ugliest. Parking lots and strip malls, empty lots and cracked sidewalks, trash heaps and construction sites transform from eye-sores into pockets of enchanted calm. No other catastrophe possesses such redeeming magic; no other disaster leaves everything in its wake *more* beautiful rather than less. Barring Calvary, that is.

The Most Powerful Woman on Wall Street

A nice metaphor, to be sure, but nothing more if it doesn't hold true in actual life. Fortunately, there exists real hope for those stuck in the seculosity of work—just not the kind you discover via more *exertion*. Surrender, sometimes willful though mostly not, is the most reliable route. The late, great theologian and food critic Robert Capon said it best when he wrote, "If the world could have lived its way to salvation, it would have, long ago. The fact is that it can only die its way there, lose its ways there."

One trenchant example of what he means would be Erin Callan, who was named "the most powerful woman on Wall Street" during her brief tenure as Chief Financial Officer of Lehman Brothers, a position she held from September 2007 to June 2008—an incredibly tumultuous period for the American economy. A few years later she described her relationship to work in vivid terms:

> I didn't start out with the goal of devoting all of myself to my job. It crept in over time. First I spent a half-hour on Sunday organizing my e-mail, to-do list and calendar to make Monday morning easier. Then I was working a few hours on Sunday, then all day. My boundaries slipped away until work was all that was left. Inevitably, when I left my job, it devastated me. I couldn't just move on. I did not know how to value who I was versus what I did. What I did *was* who I was. Without the [financial] crisis, I may never have been strong enough to step away. Perhaps I needed what felt at the time like some of the worst experiences in my life to come to a place where I could be grateful for the life I had.

Deliverance for Ms. Callan arrived under the auspices of a catastrophe, as it does for many of us.[28] It took a major recession to do for her what she could not do for herself, to interrupt her best-laid plans and reorganize her priorities. At the risk of exaggeration, the precondition for her current well-being was the death of how she conceived of herself. "Surrender" doesn't really do the ordeal justice. "Relinquishment under extreme duress" might be more accurate.

---

28. Summed up best in the words of what may be my favorite roadside church sign of all time: "When you're down to nothing, God is up to something." Amen!

The pattern here should ring some bells. What Erin describes can only be called *cruciform*, an echo of the deeper rhythm of redemption we see borne out in experiences of genuine recovery, as well as other capital-R Religious frameworks, most notably in the Easter story itself. Who was Jesus, after all, if not an inefficient healer who bore the brunt of the Roman machine? Christians believe that his passivity on the cross dignifies failures of all stripes—indeed, washes their anxious souls white as snow.

The Hope of an Unfair Boss

Not all of us encounter such dramatic circumstances—or need to—just as not everyone can be classified as a workaholic or chronic procrastinator. No matter what kind of relationship we have with work, however, we still breathe the air of a culture intoxicated with productivity and success.

Into our harried and harrying world reverberate the words of that most un-American of Christ's parables, that of the Workers in the Vineyard (Matthew 20:1–16). A landowner hires men first thing in the morning to work his vineyard, comes back to the marketplace a few hours later to hire more, then again a few hours after that, and then once more, just before the end of the day.

At sundown, he pays them all the same, a full day's wage. Those who arrived first are miffed and proceed to voice their displeasure. But the landowner stands his ground. He does not penalize anyone involved, least of all those who are most clearly (and disrespectfully) hampered by an excessive devotion to what they feel their productivity has brought them. They get the same paycheck.

Christ paints a portrait of a place where reward is not a matter of output or merit but grace, where we are valued according to our presence rather than our accomplishment, where all the boss seems to require of his workers is their need. This is unfair and offensive to the early risers but of deep comfort to those who get there late, the inefficient and unproductive.

The parable sketches a religion of hope: one in which love and esteem are not distributed on the basis of output, where men and women aren't evaluated according to how well they stack up against others, but on the largeness of divine generosity.

It may not boost the bottom line, but I'm told it *works*.

CHAPTER 6

THE SECULOSITY
OF LEISURE

My friend wasn't training for a marathon. That would have made more sense. It was Sunday, and he was about a week out from running in his first 10K race. On his route that morning, he wanted me to know, he had passed three gyms with full parking lots, five packed fitness studios, and six nearly empty churches.

Thanks for the report, I said, disingenuously. I hope you trip and fall next week. He laughed and hung up.

He hadn't called *just* to needle his religious friend. A few days previous we'd had a conversation about the burgeoning SoulCycle phenomenon. A mutual acquaintance of ours had become an instructor and kept inviting us to come down to the "Soul Sanctuary" and do a class. I was afraid of the soreness I knew would result, but my buddy took the plunge and immediately got weirded out by the overt religiosity—and this coming from a guy well acquainted with fitness fanatics.

SoulCycle may be the most popular fitness company to appeal to the spiritual aspirations of its customers—their classes even follow a discernible liturgy—but they are far from the only one.[29] Americans have been religious about exercise since Richard Simmons first started sweatin' to the oldies, but in the last decade or so, marketers have clearly gotten the memo and made the association explicit. Sunday mornings no longer present a toss-up between church and the gym; the gym now *is* church. You pay your tithe, you pass the peace, you follow the same rituals and sit under the same symbols, maybe even reach endorphin-induced transcendence, what athletes call the *zone.*

Alongside the spiritualization of exercise, a related trend has emerged: extreme exercise. Boutique outfits like CrossFit and hot yoga demand fierce commitment to extraordinarily punishing routines, promising to transform not just the body but the entire person. They are philosophies of life as much as philosophies of health, with the creeds to prove it. As such, they don't seek members but converts. Try our program and it will not only tone your abs but your personality. You'll be transformed into a healthier and happier you, the ads tell us, sounding a whole lot like televangelists. As the joke goes, how do you know if someone does Cross-Fit? Don't worry, they'll tell you.

It is no coincidence that these programs are expensive. Those with money to spare crave the burning of calories and are willing to pay a premium for pain. Think about it: if you feel guilty about your privilege, then the more intense and demoralizing the

---

29. *Liturgy* might be a strong word, but the classes do typically adhere to a predictable pattern of sitting and standing, peaks and valleys, that a repeat customer can rely upon. Instructors preside over the classes with charisma and authority, fostering an intentional sense of drama while dropping enough aphorisms about everyday life to make the participants feel like they gleaned something nonphysical, too.

activity feels, and the more it resembles hard labor, the better. Which explains why sledgehammers, truck tires, and a general lack of air conditioning feature so prominently: the debasement doubles as a form of atonement. *Puritanical* would apply if that word didn't also connote a belief in a gracious God. A better term would be *Spartan*, since the faith on offer is in one's own potential.

One of my favorite humor websites ridiculed this dynamic brilliantly in a video about a fictional new fitness tracker called the Nike Run Logic Plus, which tells a person not just how far they're running, but *why* they run. "[The Nike Run Logic Plus] pinpoints the desperate psychological demons at the root of your exercise routine," goes the pitch. The potential motivations listed by the app include "constant shame," "still single," and "disappointed father," before sharing the mock-testimonial of one user: "I'm super afraid that my friends don't really like me. I ran 27 miles today. Now I feel nothing."

So we stay glued to the wisdom of ripped zealots who encourage us to reject indulgences and seek out the glory of disciplined self-abnegation, twenty burpees at a time. Never mind that the endless measuring inherent in compulsive exercise tends to feed a person's anxiety rather than assuage it, or that physical fitness, by its daily nature, can become just as cruel and oppressive a taskmaster as anything medieval monks could have dreamt up.

The idea here is not that exercise is somehow bad. Of course not! Cutting out junk food is a fundamentally good idea, and our muscles need all the help they can get to keep pumping. Shedding a few lbs can do wonders for a person's confidence, and there is nothing wrong with feeling physically good. But there is a world of difference between exercise as good for us and exercise as salvation.

Welcome to what may be the most transparently absurd wing of contemporary righteousness: the seculosity of leisure.

The seculosity of leisure comprises those activities that occupy our downtime, not just exercise but hobbies, relaxation, play, sleep—all those sectors of human enterprise that seem most resistant to a productivity gloss. Thus the absurdity: the cult of productivity has taken captive its polar opposite, turning repose itself into a venue for scorekeeping and self-justification. The irony would be amusing, and the ingenuity impressive, were these encroachments not so effective.

Play Now!

Indoctrination into the seculosity of leisure begins well before our first workout. All you need is some playdough and alphabet blocks to get going.

Dr. Peter Gray, a psychologist at Boston College, defines play as "activity that is (1) self-chosen and self-directed; (2) intrinsically motivated; (3) structured by mental rules; (4) imaginative; and (5) produced in an active, alert, but nonstressed frame of mind." Not a means to an end, in other words, but an activity as its own reward. He goes on to report that "since about 1955 . . . children's free play has been continually declining, at least partly because adults have exerted ever-increasing control over children's activities."

Anecdotal evidence supports this. The next time you find yourself at a playground, cozy up to a parent of a young child and ask them about playtime. Odds are, they'll give you a litany about how overscheduled their kids' lives are compared to when they were growing up, how after-school extracurriculars start earlier and earlier, the requirements ever more aggressive.[30]

Talk to parents of older kids, or teenagers themselves, and you'll hear how internships and training camps are making summertime idleness a thing of the past, that vacations have become a scheduling nightmare for most families. Every few months some pundit picks up the thread and writes a shrill missive about the fallout incurred by a generation that's never had a chance to engage in activities apart from their usefulness on the good ole' college transcript. Psychologist Madeline Levine expresses the situation in stark terms: "The cost of this relentless drive to perform at unrealistically high levels is a generation of kids who resemble nothing so much as trauma victims." Ouch.

If the above sounds more like an expansion of work than a co-opting of play, have no fear, play itself is making a comeback. After decades of cutting back, many single-sex grade schools, especially the progressively minded ones, have begun doubling the amount of recess time. Books about "playful parenting" receive the full NPR treatment. Offices in Silicon Valley look more and more like jungle gyms than workspaces with each passing quarter. TED talks about the gamification of society get millions of views. And game theorists win the Nobel Prize.

You see these things and you take heart that, contra Elvis Costello, playtime is not over, that we as a culture still value it and are making sacrifices to protect it.

---

30. As mentioned in the parenting chapter, they'll likely also admit to feeling powerless to absent themselves from the vicious cycle.

Sadly, the closer you look into the resurgence of play, the harder it is to shake the suspicion that, in the name of restoring play as a vital element of childhood (and life), we are actually digging ourselves deeper into seculosity, undermining the very thing we're trying to salvage.

The most effective way to convince Americans that they should play more is not to tell them they need to work less and have more fun. To make a compelling case for playtime, you need to underline its byproducts. Lawrence Cohen's *The Art of Roughhousing*, for example, cannot resist relaying reports about how the amount and quality of roughhousing a child engages in predicts their first-grade achievement better than kindergarten test scores. And when an expert like Peter Gray highlights the relation of play to happiness (which he does, to his credit, see as the most important aspect), it's telling that he also lists the obligatory "benefits":

> Play helps children . . . learn how to make decisions, solve problems, exert self-control, and follow rules; learn to regulate their emotions; make friends and learn to get along with others as equals.

Phew! We can rest easy. Well, not *rest* exactly, but you get the idea. Play is no longer the enemy of efficiency or a willful alternative to work. It is another road to accomplishment, productive enough to warrant inclusion on the schedule of human affairs. The message is clear: Play well enough and you will increase your score. So don't mess up!

Ordering someone to have fun, of course, is a guaranteed way to ensure they don't. The second you attach a desired outcome to play, or the second it becomes a tactic or strategy for improved performance, it ceases to be play. It becomes yet another activity to put on our to-do list, another arena for success or failure, another law.

Mindful of Our Productivity

In response to the never-ending barrage of information transmitted our way, more and more of us find it useful to meditate in order to achieve any serenity. Indeed, you can't talk about how we relax today without talking about meditation's more fashionable (and nearly identical) cousin, *mindfulness*. Hokey as the term itself may be, if you look past the New Age connotations, you can see why it has become such a buzzword.

The definition of mindfulness depends on whom you ask. Speaking as someone who has found it personally helpful, here's my shot: mindfulness refers to a proven technique for re-entering the present moment and thereby experiencing reprieve from the mental projections that cause us so much suffering and stress. To be mindful involves sitting still and paying attention to the various narratives and imperatives that haunt our inner lives. It can be helpful to think of those narratives as a tape that plays in your head on repeat. It's usually some variation of not-good-enoughness, such as "if people really knew me, they'd laugh at me" or "my body is gross."

The goal of mindfulness is not to stop these judgments but purely to note them, thereby detaching ourselves from the thoughts and feelings that we confuse with reality. If it sounds like Buddhism-lite, that's because it pretty much is. Part of what makes mindfulness so appealing to so many is that it functions like a religious discipline without any reference to dogma or even the supernatural.

Various studies of mindfulness techniques in recent years have revealed a host of verifiable benefits: not just lower stress levels, but improved function of the immunity system, lower inflammation, deeper focus and clarity. It's good for you. And its meteoric rise in popularity should indicate the degree to which people feel overwhelmed, worried, and just plain unhappy—as well as the degree to which they are not finding peace in other places, like the church.

Sounds great, right? Sort of. You see, meditation has never been more stressful. The moment that mindfulness appeared to be working was the moment it became a target for seculosity, a harness for self-improvement and therefore self-justification, another instrument of credit. Today, apps like Headspace and Calm allow you to track and display the consecutive days that you've meditated, encouraging users to compete for the longest streaks. You can sign up for services that ding your credit card $10 every time you miss a session. Pavlok, a company that sells electronic shocking devices to help people change their behavior, suggests meditation as one of the top uses for its wristbands, which cost anywhere from $145 to $245. In this way, a practice designed to alleviate guilt and anxiety becomes the source of it.

"I'm fairly certain that there is no precedent for this in traditional Buddhist practice," one expert on Eastern religion commented. "Many monks meditate every day for decades, and I have never heard of anyone keeping track." This is because competitive meditation is a contradiction in terms.

There's more. Companies like insurance giant Aetna have recently jumped on the train, instituting an employee mindfulness program, which has reportedly saved about "$2,000 per employee in health-care costs, and gained about $3,000 per employee in *productivity*." An umbrella of wellness masks the company's true concern, which is the financial bottom line. Perform, perform, perform!

This is both dispiriting and impressive. Mindfulness, with its emphasis on the present rather than the future, being not doing, epitomizes the opposite of productivity. The only way to ensure that it won't relax you is to demand that it do so—that is, that it *produce* such-and-such a result.

What we have here is a textbook example of how a spiritual practice becomes a religious one, something helpful turns into something justifying, something grace-based sours into something legalistic. It mirrors the way that many Christians experience regular churchgoing or individual quiet times. What starts out as a respite turns into a ladder.

This doesn't mean that a mindful brain isn't a whole lot happier and more peaceful than a distractedly anxious one. It just means that the real disease isn't fatigue but sin.

Striving in Our Sleep

Remarkable as its other accomplishments may be, the seculosity of leisure hits peak absurdity in its annexation of sleep. I'm serious.

In late 2014, the Centers for Disease Control and Prevention (CDC) declared insomnia to be a full-blown health epidemic in the United States. Americans are having more trouble sleeping than ever before, and the number of diagnosed sleep disorders has skyrocketed.

You might think this news would correlate to problems in the sleep industry. If their products were more popular—if they were reaching consumers—people would be sleeping better, not worse. But the exact opposite is true.

Over the past decade or so, the sleep industry has blossomed over into a $32 billion per year endeavor. In addition to electronic sleep trackers like the Fitbit, you can buy sleep-inducing chocolates, macromolecularly engineered beds-in-a-box, technologically enhanced sleep masks, and all manner of white noise machines, not to mention an ever-increasing variety of pharmaceuticals. The number one paid app on iTunes in the Spring of 2014—in every G-8 country—was the Sleep Cycle Alarm Clock, which delivers "optimized rest" by monitoring its owner's REMs and waking them only during a light phase of their cycle. Sleep is no longer a niche market.

Essayist Eve Fairbanks credits the rapid expansion to a wider shift in the culture:

> If this onslaught of coverage has an underlying ideology, it is this: First, that sleep is absolutely critical for high performance; and second, that you can improve your sleep—but only with intense effort. . . . We want to sleep more now not because we value sleep more on its own terms, but because we are so fixated on productivity.

Rest is now just prelude to more work, not a respite from stress but something else to stress over, another area where you may be falling short, another wrench in the self-justification toolkit.[31] It's enough to make a person want to take a nap.

If there's any comfort here, it is that when you're asleep you are unconscious; "intention" can only have so much impact. Sleep is still sleep, regardless of how it's advertised.

---

31. Case in point: one of the *New York Times*' most popular articles on the subject of somnolence was Tony Schwartz's column in November of 2013 titled, no joke, "Relax! You'll Be More Productive."

Scapegoating the Treadmill

We could discuss plenty of other forms of leisure through the lens of seculosity. We could talk, for instance, about creativity and how intertwined that word has become with the solving of problems and making of money as opposed to flights of fancy. Or we could mention how efficiency experts like Cal Newport have begun praising "laziness" as a key to better intellectual processing, citing astrophysicist Stephen Hawking as an example. Or we could explore the observation that no one seems to have hobbies anymore.[32] But the bottom line would be the same: the cult of productivity is real, its demands excessive, and its reach expanding to the point of farcicality.

And yet, as with all targets of seculosity, it would be equally absurd to conclude that productivity itself is to blame. In order for a society to function—in order for an individual to survive—things need to get done. Steps need to be taken, calories burned, money earned, results produced.

We run into problems, as we always do, when the work(s)-based mentality that our vocations rightly demand subsumes every other sector of life. If we never get a break, we grow bitter and brittle. Joy evaporates. We begin to view others as means to an end, not people with the same needs and vulnerabilities as us. Plus, the treadmill of "always-on" productivity enslaves us to our utility, which will invariably diminish as we get older. Once the trajectory

---

32. Side-hustles, extracurriculars, ongoing projects and pursuits, yes, but not hobbies. At least not in the sense of something you do just for the sake of enjoyment and to pass the time, i.e., independent of excellence or praise. Kite-flying and model trains and that sort of thing.

of our life-stats starts heading downward, we all know where it ends—past the playground, in the graveyard.

Fortunately, there are worse places to be than surrounded by symbols of heavenly rest. We may find that, considering the inroads made by the cult of productivity, the good news emblazoned on so many tombstones shines that much brighter.

May the Fourth Be with You

Given our conflicted relationship with leisure, one can understand why theologian Walter Brueggemann considers the Fourth Commandment—the one that mandates Sabbath rest—to be "the most difficult and most urgent of commandments in our society." He's not referring to the fact that the fourth gets the most ink of all the commandments, in both Deuteronomy and Exodus, even though it does. He's referring to soccer game schedules, twenty-four-hour gyms, and all those things that make our culture such a fundamentally restless one. He is concerned with the ever-mounting challenges faced by anyone who might be so bold as to take the Sinai injunction seriously.

The roots of the Fourth Commandment warrant our attention. Both accounts of its announcement underline a departure from the slavery that the Israelites experienced while in Egypt. Pharaoh was more than an anxious ruler, he was a self-proclaimed deity singularly focused on productivity and hard work. He viewed the Israelites as a labor force, nothing more—no water breaks and no dignity.

Freed from the yolk of Egyptian tyranny, Moses's words to his fellow Israelites in Deuteronomy ring out as follows:

Remember that you were a slave in the land of Egypt, and the Lord your God brought you out from there with a mighty hand and an outstretched arm; therefore the Lord your God commanded you to keep the sabbath day. (Deuteronomy 5:15)

God goes to great pains to remind the Israelites that they are no longer slaves, and therefore no longer synonymous with their utility. Rest would be what would distinguish this new regime.

This only makes our current situation more ironic. I remember my grandfather telling me about his childhood Sundays and how frustrating it was that they weren't allowed to do much. To kids in his generation, Sabbath meant no baseball, no movies, no shopping. It did not connote freedom so much as a resounding No, an inflexible law put there to confound fun. What was intended for good had hardened into a mode of control and repression—what religious people might describe as legalism. The spirit had been lost, as it often is.

Today, the zeitgeist has shifted. What was once prohibition might now be heard as permission: to stop, take a breath, and remember that we are more than what we produce, more than our job title or bank balance. Sabbath, in this light, does indeed represent resistance to the dominating paradigm of more, more, more—an invitation to the experience of grace. As if we needed more proof that God is not an American, Brueggemann writes:

The alternative on offer [in the Sabbath] is the awareness and practice of the claim that we are situated on the receiving end of the gifts of God. To be so situated is a staggering option, because we are accustomed to being on the initiating end of all things. We neither expect nor even want a gift to be given, so inured are we to accomplishing and achieving and possessing.

And yet, lest we mistake law for grace, the Fourth Commandment is still a part of the Decalogue. Tempting as it may be, a louder, more articulate expression of divinely *or* culturally mandated rest will not inspire repose in those for whom productivity has become a replacement religion.

Just think about all the times when you've been told to "just relax." Was relaxation your first reaction?

If you are one of those rare beasts who answers in the affirmative, then poll your Type A neighbors on what they do to unwind. They'll more than likely give you a list of reasons why downtime isn't an option right now. They may even do what many well-meaning Christians do: embrace a mandatory day of rest while dodging its existential punch by finding another, more ostensibly holy pursuit to occupy them on their day off. They simply replace one form of self-justification with another. Instead of making a contribution at our desk, we make a contribution on our bicycle, or with our kids, or at our church. Anything but sit still ("and know that I am God"!).

There's a line in the Psalms where the seculosity of leisure and the cult of productivity are addressed more or less head-on: "It is in vain that you rise up early and go late to rest, eating the bread of anxious toil; for [the Lord] gives sleep to his beloved" (Psalm 127:2).

Later you have Jesus himself, who never related to people on the basis of their productivity. If anything, he reserved his time for those whose contribution to society seemed dubious at best. He went so far as to make them his friends.

In one memorable episode, those who follow Christ are referred to as "sheep without a shepherd," hurrying this way and that, doing God knows what (Matthew 9:36). The evangelist tells us that instead of judging these people for running around aimlessly or shouting at them to "just relax" or learn to rest better, he has compassion for them. He doesn't wait for them to calm down or figure out their aversion to leisure before he engages. Nor does he leave them in a trap of unremitting activity. Instead, he begins to teach. And what he teaches them—and later what he embodies—is that the judgment we're all so afraid of, the one that undergirds our restlessness, has been quelled, once for all.

We may be meting out comfort to ourselves on the basis of our efforts, but the rest Jesus conveys stems from how God sees us, not how we see ourselves. Justification by faith is the fancy term, and it is commonly associated with a certain German monk who understood these things far better than me. In fact, he was able to sum up this entire chapter in a few sentences back in the 1530s:

> It is impossible to gain peace of conscience by the methods and means of the world. Experience proves this. Various holy orders have been launched for the purpose of securing peace of conscience through religious exercises, but they proved failures because such devices only increase doubt and despair. We find no rest for our weary bones unless we cling to the word of grace.

Amen. Or should I say: Namaste, sleep tight, and may the fourth be with you.

CHAPTER 7

THE SECULOSITY
OF FOOD

I n one of his most popular stand-up bits, comedian Jim Gaffigan relates the story of bumping into an acquaintance at McDonald's. The run-in catches both men off guard, and in lieu of saying hello, the other man offers a hasty explanation, "Uh, I'm only here for the ninety-nine-cent ATM. What are *you* doing, Jim?"

Before he can collect himself, Jim says he's there to meet a prostitute, definitely not to eat anything. Heaven forbid!

We laugh, but the observation isn't baseless. The shame is well known to those of us who make sure fast-food containers aren't visible through our car windows, or anyone who pays for a milkshake in cash to avoid having to explain the expense to a spouse later.

Jim's choice of substitute vice isn't arbitrary. Much of the moralism and anxiety that once surrounded the bedroom now focuses on the kitchen. We talk about food today the way we used to talk about sex. The last time you used the word *cheat*, for instance, was it in reference to a broken vow or something you ate? I'd wager the latter.

The shift is relatively recent. To my grandparents' generation, the way that we now talk about food—the *amount* we talk about it—is hard to fathom. They may have witnessed the health-food crazes of the 1970s and watched Julia Child on PBS, but nothing could have prepared them for the full-fledged religion of food we have today.

A hefty slice of the seculosity of food falls under the category of "foodie culture," the most obvious expressions of which have to be the rise of celebrity chefs and the explosion of food television. Self-proclaimed foodies make pilgrimages, sometimes across continents, to eat at a certain chef's table. And then there's the advent of twenty-four-hour cooking television. Ina Garten, Nigella Lawson, and David Chang are probably the most well-known names, but new stars are rising every day. Moreover, what used to be a single genre now encompasses several: reality cooking shows like *Top Chef* and *A Chef's Life*, game shows like *Chopped* and *Iron Chef*, documentary-style prestige series like *The Mind of a Chef*, entire channels—plural!—full of this stuff.

I joke with my wife that we now watch more cooking-related television than *non*-cooking-related television. It's very relaxing— as long as you don't watch on an empty stomach.

Television is only the tip of the iceberg. We also have more choices of what to eat than ever before. I grew up in a world—and I'm not that old—where there was no such thing as organic food. You didn't go to the grocery store and make a conscious choice between organic milk and the regular kind. It was milk or nothing.

We also source our food more broadly than ever before, which may seem like freedom but all too often translates into anxiety.

You're not eating at McDonald's, sure, but where are you getting your groceries? Kroger? Wegmans? Trader Joe's? Or maybe you're shopping local. But if so, how local are you going to go? The farmer's market? The farm itself? Canvas your neighbors and you'll find that grocery store loyalties run deep. The implication is clear: eating habits inform our identity, and differences are not morally neutral. There *is* a right answer to these questions.

Hungry for Salvation

Some critics suggest that food has replaced art as an outlet of high culture in the West. "Food now expresses the symbolic values and absorbs the spiritual energies of the educated class," observed author William Deresiewicz. "It has become invested with the meaning of life. It is seen as the path to salvation for the self and humanity, both."

Indeed, our national conversation about food is soaked in religious language. You cannot talk about something like fasting without invoking some notion of righteousness.

I choose that example intentionally. A practice once reserved for monks and gurus has become something regular folks brag about on social media. We just call it a cleanse now—which only makes our motivation more transparent. We are cleaning out our insides, purging the toxins, purifying our systems and ourselves, one glass of cayenne lemonade at a time.

The seculosity of food holds that the cure to our ennui does not lie in a book or at a church but in a different aisle at the supermarket. Find the right ingredient, or set of ingredients, and you can become who you were meant to be. Stick with the wrong ones and you have only yourself to blame for your unhappiness. All who are lost need only pledge adherence to the One True Diet that promises a new self, an enlightened understanding, an abundant life. And no diet is complete without its appointed prophet, some leader who has paved the way by word and example, its Dr. Atkins or Michael Pollan in whom we can place our faith.

Indeed, there exists very little difference today between aspirational eating and aspirational *living*. Take Hollywood dynamo Gwyneth Paltrow for example. Her lifestyle brand, Goop, grew from a no-frills e-newsletter into a $250 million/year business over ten short years by virtue of its central commandment: do this and you will become like Gwyneth.[33] There are clothes to purchase and workouts to do, but more than anything, Goop shows women (and their soon-to-be sugar-free families) what to eat. The first three cookbooks flew off the shelves fast enough to make Martha Stewart's head spin.

It sounds far-fetched perhaps, until we consider the unquestioned moralism surrounding food in our culture. We dance around moral categories when it comes to other conventional vices, like sex and money, but not around food. We say things like, "Oh I was *bad*, I had a brownie," or "I'm not eating that tonight, I'm being *good*." Good and bad are much stronger terms than healthy and unhealthy. Before long we've moved from the piece of food itself being good or bad, to the person eating it being good or bad, completing the short slide from morality into moralism.

Food has also become heavily politicized. The writer Alice Waters once went so far as to say that "every single choice we make about food matters, at every level. The right choice saves the

---

33. Of course, the commercial success of the Goop brand depends on the impossibility of fulfilling this commandment, i.e., on the erstwhile Margot Tenenbaum remaining in a class by herself.

world." An incredibly strong statement to make about anything, let alone caloric intake. Presumably she had ecological issues in mind—how far we can stretch and sustain earth's resources—but again, previous generations would not have located her sentiment on the continuum of sanity. (Which may not be a criterion for dismissing such claims, but should still give us pause.)

Put in less grandiose terms, we feel judged for our food choices, and we are right to feel that way because we *are* being judged for our food choices. No wonder we apologize so often for what we eat. "I'm so sorry I'm eating this right now; please look the other way while I pound this burger."

Yet we also feel loved for our food choices. It used to be you knew someone if you knew what they liked to eat. Today, you know someone if you know what they *cannot* eat, their food allergies and dietary stipulations.

Perhaps it should come as no surprise that, given the value we now place on food, meals have come to function for many of us as a daily and sometimes hourly drama of discipline, deprivation, and self-satisfaction, or conversely, indulgence and guilt. Our inner monologues after the menu arrives at our restaurant table resembles nothing so much as that of Saint Augustine passing by an attractive woman on the streets of Hippo. If we make the "bad choice," we atone for yesterday's extravagance by withholding something tasty today. The price must be paid, preferably an emotional as well as nutritional one. The piety on display is not hidden.

Again, for those caught up in the seculosity of food, diet is no longer what we put in our mouths. It is a meticulous scoresheet of personal and social righteousness, the measure by which we determine our own value and other people's. I dare say diet has become a more reliable indicator of social class in America than bank balance or zip code.

Orthorexics Anonymous

The point here is not to suggest that food is unimportant or innocuous. What and how we eat has real consequences. Some foodstuffs are better for us than others. There are deeply important ethical questions to be answered about where we get our meals from, about how we harvest our crops and treat our animals, about who benefits and in what ways. Increased awareness around such topics should be applauded and encouraged.

Plus, cooking represents an avenue of tremendous creativity, beauty, and artistic expression. Social cohesion too: across cultures, meals provide one of the best opportunities for people to be together, to spend time with those we love, and to get to know each other better. Most of all, food is delicious! And that pleasure is no small thing in a world filled with heartache and scarcity.

But when someone pays close to twelve dollars for a small bottle of green juice, nutrition, connection, and taste are not the only draws. We are buying more than novelty or even status. We are bartering for purity, wholeness, and immortality. We are climbing a ladder to the heavens. Diet has become the justifying story of our lives.

Unfortunately, as with other areas of performancism, we find that the ladder only gets longer the higher we climb. What promises to deliver health ends up coughing up the opposite, the most pathological example being the eating disorder on the rise known as *Orthorexia nervosa*, a term that literally means "fixation on righteous eating." The website of the National Eating

Disorders Association describes the condition in remarkably religious terms:

> Orthorexia starts out as an innocent attempt to eat more healthfully, but orthorexics become fixated on food quality and purity. . . . Every day is a chance to eat right, be "good," rise above others in dietary prowess, and self-punish if temptation wins (usually through stricter eating, fasts and exercise). Self-esteem becomes wrapped up in the purity of orthorexics' diet and they sometimes feel superior to others, especially in regard to food intake.

The obsessive parsing of which foods are "good" and which are "bad" means orthorexics often end up malnourished. And even if they remain healthy, eating becomes so stressful that their personal relationships come under pressure and social isolation ensues.[34]

Of course, you don't have to suffer from a diagnosable disorder to be familiar with the self-obsession that results when we monitor our diet too closely.[35] It doubles as the physical equivalent of the compulsive pulse-taking that occurs in spiritual environments that emphasize personal transformation. It's hard to love or serve another person if you cannot take your eyes off your utensils.

---

34. Don't take my word for it: google "vegan YouTube drama" and buckle your seatbelt.
35. What a cruel irony that many of us who "eat our feelings" are—counterproductively—trying to *get away* from ourselves.

The Worst F-Word There Is

Maybe I haven't convinced you yet. Maybe you're of a mind that the extra attention around food today is warranted, that few people take it all *that* seriously, and while some activists may go overboard, calling our collective relationship with food a religion seems like hyperbole.

I've got one more arrow in my quiver, and it has to do with the most taboo F-word in the English language: F-A-T. The word is so loaded, in fact, that I only feel safe using it in reference to myself.

When I was in middle school, my grandmother sat me down and told me that unlike my two brothers, I would have to watch what I ate as I got older. I don't know what tipped her off, whether it was my husky build or awful snacking habits, but she wanted me to know that if I didn't pay attention to what I ate, I could develop a problem, the one known as *fatness*.

She was frank, but she was right. The truth is, I've always looked to food for comfort, especially during times of stress. Ben and Jerry's, not Budweiser, is my preferred method of self-medication.

And so, every June of adulthood, I've undertaken a month-long "reduction" in which I cut out desserts and carbs and late-night nibbles. For men my age, the pounds fall off with relatively little effort and old pants soon begin to fit again. Affirmation starts to flow my way in the form of unsolicited comments (which my inner lawyer immediately flips into condemnation, i.e., "had I really gotten so heavy?"). I start to feel a bit better, both physiologically and emotionally. Your body thanks you, as they say. The social rewards can be pretty noticeable, too, even for a guy. No more pizza-neck!

Yet the downsides are not negligible. For thirty days it's tunnel vision all the way, as I place my needs and plans above those of my wife, kids, and coworkers. I can't seem to do it any other way. All to avoid the accusation of F-A-T.

The self-centeredness pales in comparison to the self-righteousness. The moment I step on the scale and it registers less is the moment I reproach both my past self for being lazy and others for their failure to be as disciplined as I am. I become what journalist Joyce Wadler calls a "Dieting Supremacist" or we might call a Food Pharisee, forgetting the many factors that contributed to my weight loss, as well as the inconvenient fact that I gained it all back the last time. Instead I craft a narrative about self-determination and effort and performance. A testimony, if you will.

The swiftness of this change in attitude, and the size of the feelings involved, reveals just how much I lean on my relationship to food (and by extension, body image) for self-esteem and justification. Still, given the choice between being a self-aggrandizing performancist who can fit into his clothes and a self-loathing performancist who can't, I choose the former. Neither is what we might call spiritually healthy, but the latter at least reinforces need rather than self-sufficiency.

Back to the dreaded F-Word. I remember when my kids were younger, overhearing one of them ask a babysitter why she was fat. The air in the room froze. You could almost hear the screech of car brakes and the scratch of a needle across vinyl. It was as though we were in a Victorian novel and someone had blasphemed. The babysitter handled it graciously, thank God, but my wife and I were incredibly embarrassed, ten times more so than if he'd used a different f-word. We gave her triple the usual tip.

The situation came to mind a few months later, when the popular radio show *This American Life* aired an episode called "Tell Me I'm Fat." The opening segment presented an interview that host Ira Glass conducted with writer and self-described "fat person" Lindy West. Her responses were pertinent:

> The way that we are taught to think about fatness is that fat is not a permanent state. You're just a thin person who's failing consistently for your whole life. . . . So to actually say, OK, I am fat—and I have been as long as I can remember, so I don't know why I live in this imaginary future where someday I'm going to be thin.

No doubt it's an indication of the moral import we have given this issue that West's words raise our hackles immediately. Hold on a second, we say, let's not get carried away and pretend as though being fat is somehow okay—or justified. Sure, it's nice if people can accept themselves, but that doesn't mean there aren't serious health concerns involved. Biology follows certain rules, after all, and we haven't even mentioned the political or financial ramifications.

However you frame the offense, West has transgressed a tacit but firm cultural commandment, failing the litmus test of cultural righteousness. Such heresy is rarely tolerated, even among the staunchly tolerant. A world engorged on performancism cannot distinguish between the number on the scale and the person standing on it.

Weightism is a natural byproduct of a culture that has absolutized food and eating. This truth becomes even more unavoidable toward the end of that same radio show, when reporter Daniel Engber tells the story of the controversial "Pounds Off Plan" adopted at Oral Roberts University, a strictly Christian institution, in the early 1970s. The college prohibited overweight students from graduating until they met a certain body-fat percentage.

Administrators canceled the program fairly soon after its inauguration, realizing the fundamental dissonance with their insistence that God valued the heart over the waistline.

Engber notes the irony that a similar renunciation did not take place in the secular sphere. If anything, the nation's spare religiosity had found a suitable anchor:

> Born again by losing weight. The newscasters [on *The Today Show*] made it seem like this was some crazy Christian thing. But it wasn't really all that strange . . . by the mid-'70s, diet plans were as ubiquitous as they are today. Then, as now, being fat was not just seen by lots of people as a medical failing, but a moral one.

A Few Key Ingredients

Food has always been linked to religion. Kosher laws in Judaism are wide-ranging, same with those that govern what's considered Halal in Islam. Hindus do not eat cows. If you read the New Testament, you'll find mentions of food everywhere. Christ ministered to people over meals. For many Christians around the world, breaking of bread and sipping of wine form the heart of their weekly worship. So food is not somehow a religion-free zone that has recently been co-opted by a select few.

The innovation of the last twenty years is to make food a religion unto itself. I have several theories as to why and how this happened.

First, food is tempting as a religious object because of the control it affords, whether that be over our bodies or, more often than not, emotions. "Comfort food" isn't just hearty cuisine, it's food used to dole out an emotional reward, for example a candy bar after a long day. In this sense, food represents a sincere attempt to meet a core need, the need for love. As such, it can also be a way to (re)enforce perceived lovelessness. I'm referring to those who resist meals in order to punish themselves—to make themselves feel bad or look as bad as they feel.

Next, there's the moral appeal itself. In the vacuum left by the decline of Religion, we crave some area of life where terms like *good* and *bad* still apply, and where we can agree on their meaning. And despite other divergences of outlook, we can generally agree on what constitutes a well-cooked and a poorly cooked steak. We can say, "That is a *good* tomato, and that is not." Thus food becomes an area of public discourse where objectivity is still allowed to thrive, where moral categories have not been explained away by context or brick-walled by their political implications. We love this; it implies a sense of order, security, and control.

Finally, food is tempting as an object of seculosity because of its tie to mortality. We believe that if we eat the right things, we will live longer and with a higher quality of life. As the nutritionists remind us, there is plenty of science to support this reasoning. Furthermore, if there's any merit to those fashionable theories that cast all religion as an attempt to deal with our finitude, then food would play an increasingly important role as the plausibility of God diminishes across our culture.

Of course, if Keith Richards of the Rolling Stones has taught us anything, it's that longevity does not necessarily correlate to healthy lifestyle or purity of intake. People with impeccable eating habits die all the time, and gluttons can live long lives. Robert Capon once wrote that "the last secret of the cult of nutrition—the mystery to be guarded at all costs—is that the implicit promise of immortality is bunk. The idol in the innermost sanctum doesn't just have no clothes, it isn't even there."

As with all aspects of seculosity, these theories boil down to control. If food has the power not only to preserve but validate and even elevate our lives, then we merely need to figure out the right things to consume and keep to them. Such an outside-in approach to suffering puts the keys to managing our lives, our fears, our identities, our problems, or what Christians call sin, in our own hands. We have to believe that it *is* what goes into a person that defiles and defines him, not what comes out (contra Jesus in Mark 7), because the alternative—what some call faith—is too scary.

Sadly, whether at Whole Foods or Golden Corral, the garden of Eden or the upper room, the old adage holds, er, weight: what we seek to control all too often ends up controlling us.

You Are What You Eat?

The temptation to absolutize food—to ascribe to it not just nutritional but existential value—is nothing new. The New Testament reveals that food was a source of supreme anxiety and division among members of the early Christian church in Corinth. Its members were particularly concerned with whether eating meat that had been sacrificed to pagan idols—meat that was cheaper to purchase—jeopardized a person's spiritual standing.

In his first letter to that community, Paul of Tarsus spelled out an unequivocally nonperformancist approach: "Food will not bring us close to God. We are no worse off if we do not eat, and no better off if we do" (1 Corinthians 8:8). To Paul, food did not occupy a place of ultimate importance. In his view, the god the

Corinthians were trying to appease with their eating habits—the god of outside-in—did not exist.

Children know this instinctively. I remember telling one of my sons when he was five years old that if he ate any more clementines, he was going to turn into one. Maybe someone told you that when you were a kid. It's a pretty common parenting tactic. This was the first time I'd used the line on him, and not for a second did he believe me. In fact, he thought it was the funniest thing he'd ever heard. "I'm not going to turn into a clementine!"

My son knew something that we who are consumed by the seculosity of food have forgotten. We are *not* what we eat. And that is good news.

Yet, Paul did not denigrate food so much as reverse the math. He was able to do this because of the content of the Religion he espoused, which has at its center a person who loved to eat, Jesus himself. The food itself may not have been the point, per se, but the people certainly were. And as far as I can tell, none of the seats at his table went to those who felt they *deserved* them.

When they sat down together, Jesus didn't relate to his fellow diners according to their shameful failures or unbearable successes at controlling their cravings. He didn't deliver a pep talk on the benefits of courageous self-acceptance either. Perhaps because he knew they hadn't gotten there by accident. Their appetites—for love and hope, for absolution and gluten—had brought them.

Word has it, no one walked away hungry.

CHAPTER 8

THE SECULOSITY
OF POLITICS

'm. In. Loooooove," announces Elaine Benes just as Jerry Seinfeld opens the door to his apartment in a classic scene from the sitcom that bore his last name. Elaine bounds in, giddy to the point of bouncing, telling her friend, "This is it, Jerry. He's *such* an incredible person. He's real, he's honest, he's unpretentious. I'm so lucky!"

"Uh huh," Jerry responds, in typically detached fashion. "And what's his stand on . . . abortion?" By this point Elaine is seated on the couch, applying some lipstick. The second the A-word comes out of Jerry's mouth, she smears the lipstick all over her face, body language instantly seizing up.

After a moment's shock, she ventures hopefully, "Well, I'm *sure* he's pro-choice."

"How do you know?" Jerry asks.

"Because he, well. He's just so good-*looking*," Elaine offers, unconvincingly.

You can guess what happens next. Elaine and her new boy-friend find themselves on opposing sides of a Big Issue about which they both feel strongly. Crushed, she breaks off the relationship, cursing Jerry for prodding while knowing she cannot be with someone who doesn't see eye-to-eye with her on *Roe v. Wade*.

The writers play the situation for laughs, but little did they know how prophetic the scene would prove. When it was filmed in the nineties, the idea that politics could be such a clear and immediate deal-breaker between potential (soul)mates still seemed funny. It's not that people then didn't disagree fervently over such matters, just that Elaine's single-mindedness was comical—another example of the characters in that show sabotaging their chances at love.

What once looked like exaggeration has become the new normal. According to every metric available, our society has never been more divided by politics. We are less likely than ever before to have friends who vote differently from us, and more likely to choose where we live based on how our neighbors vote. In the late 1950s, when American parents were asked how they would feel if their child were to marry someone from another political party, fewer than 10 percent indicated that it would be a problem for them. In 2010, that number had more than quadrupled to roughly 40 percent.[36] God only knows what it would be today.

This makes sense when you consider that reports of party-based antipathy more than doubled among both Democrats and Republicans between 1994 and 2014. At the same time, the average

---

36. By way of contrast, when respondents in 1958 were polled on the prospect of marrying outside one's race, only 4 percent approved. By 2012 that number had risen to nearly 90 percent. Our acceptable prejudgments haven't disappeared so much as morphed.

Republican has moved to the right, ideologically, and the average Democrat to the left, leaving an ever-waning number of people with moderate or mixed political views.[37]

Nothing about this should come as a shock. Politics is well on its way to becoming the most entrenched and impermeable social divide in America, surpassing religion, income bracket, and even race. Each passing year we retreat further into ideological echo chambers.

With the possible exception of career, politics has become today's most popular replacement religion, certainly the one with the most forward momentum and cultural currency. For many, its substitution for Religion has been seamless, hardly even noticeable.

I was wearing plastic fangs and white face-paint when this hit home for me.

In the university town where my family and I live, rallies, protests, and fundraisers, usually of the left-leaning variety, are commonplace. People care about the Issues and aren't afraid to let their colors fly. While the displays occasionally induce some eye-rolling, it's preferable to apathy or suppression.

Cut to Halloween 2016, less than two weeks before the presidential election. I'm dressed up as Dracula and trick-or-treaters are descending on our neighborhood in droves, as they do every year. Kids are parading in the street, mine included, shouting and carrying on as house after house fills their bags with candy.

---

37. Over the past twenty years, the number of Americans in the "tails" of this ideological distribution has doubled from 10 percent to 21 percent. Meanwhile, the center has shrunk: today 39 percent currently take a roughly equal number of liberal and conservative positions. That is down from about half (49 percent) of the public in surveys conducted in 1994 and 2004.

All the houses but one. Of the sixty or so homes in our immediate vicinity, about fifteen boasted election-related signs out front. Yet only a single yard advocated Making America Great Again.

As we passed by that address, the adults in our crew exchanged knowing looks. Folks had been whispering about this place for weeks, scandalized. I watched as a few moms and dads steered their progeny onward. One of the kids who did venture up to the door asked the owners if there was something wrong with them.

The election results would reveal that our neighbor's political views did not lie outside the mainstream. Yet for all intents and purposes, their house was haunted. I felt like I was in a black-and-white Christmas movie, and we were shuffling past the one house in town with a menorah out front. These people did not belong.

Even a Transylvanian could see the truth: if once upon a time we looked to politics primarily for governance, we now look to it for belonging, righteousness, meaning, and deliverance—in other words, all the things for which we used to rely on Religion.[38] Understanding politics as an ersatz religion is the key not only to surviving our increasingly fractured world but finding compassion for those in its thrall, including ourselves.

A Disclaimer

It bears repeating that, like every target of seculosity, politics is a good and necessary part of life. After all, *politics* simply refers to systems of governance and the power dynamics inherent to them.

---

38. Studies even indicate that religious identity now follows political affiliation, rather than vice versa (which has been the pattern in the US historically). Meaning that, for more and more people, political convictions shape their religious beliefs, not the other way around.

The questions involved—for example, which laws to ratify and how to enforce them—deserve our sustained attention and care. They warrant our emotional investment as well. Lives often hang in the balance.

Not that we could expunge politics from our day-to-day if we wanted to. Some kind of political arrangement is necessary for humans to live together, even when it's not formalized. The exercise of power cannot be avoided if you want to relate to other people, full stop.

I should know. When friends would talk politics in college, I usually maintained that I was *apolitical*. What I meant was that, when it came to the GOP versus DNC, Republican versus Democrat, I was indifferent. Sounds sacrilegious today, and maybe those were tamer times, but I could see pluses and minuses to both parties' positions—and a whole lot of similarities. The mechanics of policy-making didn't captivate me, and I was happy to leave the nitty gritty to others and keep my energy focused on finding a girlfriend.

I no longer say that. Not because I've had some radical political awakening, but because common usage of the word has shifted—a measure, incidentally, of just how much the seculosity of politics has spread in recent years. Today, to claim that you're apolitical means that you believe yourself to be a person whose life isn't informed and shaped by power dynamics—thus revealing that you benefit from those power dynamics to the extent that you're not aware of them. In this current sense, no one is apolitical, in the same way that no one is a-cultural or a-religious. If you are alive, you are those things—the only question is *how*.

When the question of political leaning comes my way nowadays, I mutter something about being "nonpartisan" and wait for the subject to change. It can be pretty uncomfortable, not unlike telling a Christian you don't believe in God.

Politics and religion have always been close, if uneasy, cousins. Growing up in the 1980s, I associated religion with the conservative side of the political spectrum. Movements like the Moral Majority and the Religious Right explicitly tied party affiliation to faith. Good Christians vote Republican, and all that. The whole thing could not have miscarried more completely, especially when it came to the next generation(s). I'd wager that a disproportionate number of those now on the radical left grew up Baptist.

Then a few years went by and it became clear that the American right didn't have a monopoly on religiosity in politics. Perhaps it was hearing about the French Revolution in high-school history class and my jaw dropping open when we came to the section on the Cult of the Supreme Being that Robespierre set up to quicken de-Christianization in nineteenth-century France. Or it could have been studying World War II in college and stumbling across pictures of worship services held by the so-called German Christians, in which Nazi flags flanked church altars. Or maybe the revelation came during a procrastination session at the office googling Soviet propaganda and seeing the extent to which the Bolsheviks borrowed religious symbolism and rhetoric. Then again, it was probably a natural result of watching the election cycle enough times to weary of people projecting messianic hopes onto some poor soul who cannot possibly bear the weight.

Politicians throughout history, from both ends of the ideological spectrum, have made conscious efforts to channel religious devotion into nationalistic fervor as a means of consolidating power. Just as often, a desperate populace has done the work for them.

Our current form of seculosity has a slightly different makeup, though. It's no longer the nation-state cast as higher power, or a certain leader enshrined as holy, but politics itself.

The seculosity of politics is what happens when the political becomes not one lens among many for understanding the world (e.g., the metaphysical, the psychological, the spiritual) but the only one. Or the only one that matters.

Exactly what accounts for this engulfing, I'm not sure. My pet theory is that political commitment, especially on the left, has become a measure of moral character in the way that religious devotion used to be. Doubtless it also reflects a failure of other stories to captivate the popular imagination, the decline of Religion most of all. Regardless of how we've gotten here, the end result is a world in which everything is politicized. Not just how you vote, but how you shop, how you eat, how you socialize, how you vacation, and even how you worship. While it's possible to ascribe power dynamics to each one of these pursuits (and draw out their broader social implications), the suggestion that there are plenty of other ways of explaining human behavior besides politics, some of them potentially more profound, seems increasingly, well, heretical.

I remember speaking about this to a literature professor at a prestigious college. She said that in her three decades of teaching, the level of political engagement on campus had never been higher than post-2016. Much of this she saw as laudable and even exciting. Sure, she fessed to teaching a few overzealous kids who saw it as their mission to police their instructors' political convictions, but most of those reports, she insisted, were overblown. The apathy of the previous generation had gone the way of the rotary telephone and along with it, the debilitating inwardness of slackerdom. Today, passion rules. Ideas matter. Activism is the name of the game.

The main challenge at present, she told me, was encouraging her students to think in terms other than those of power—to allow a text to speak about its own concerns, rather than sift it through a preexisting ideology; to sit *below* it and learn, rather than above it and judge. She felt like she'd succeeded at the end of the semester if she'd given her students another language—*any* other—to speak in addition to that of oppressors and victims. Easier said than done.

When a Story Isn't Just a Story

Let's back up. There's a good reason why people avoid talking about politics and religion at parties, and it's not just that both subjects evoke strong emotions, which they do. We avoid talking about religion and politics in social settings for the same reason they make such frequent bedfellows. Both religion and politics traffic in all-encompassing narratives. Both attempt to make sense of, well, everything—not just the way things are but the way things should be, the way *we* are and should be, the whys and the wherefores and the so-what's. It's the opposite of relaxing territory, conversation-wise. If you want to make a good impression, probably best to stick to less ambitious topics like HGTV marathons or why no one drives stick-shift anymore.

It's worth dwelling on this word *narrative* for a moment. Someone once called us a storytelling species, and you can see why. Just think of how we spend our free time—reading the news, (binge-) watching TV, or speculating about our favorite sports team's chances this year. These are all ways of consuming and participating in stories. The same goes for our emotional lives. It's virtually impossible to talk about ourselves or the world without crafting some kind of narrative, usually one of progress and improvement but sometimes one of shame and defeat. Maybe our capacity for telling stories is what separates us from the animals. Who knows?

Yet the stories we tell are never *just* stories.

No one has done more in recent years to understand our narrative obsession—both the benefits and blind spots—than moral psychologist Jonathan Haidt. In his aptly titled book *The Righteous Mind*, he lays out something he calls Moral Foundations Theory.

According to Haidt's research, the human psyche instinctually seeks righteousness. And the righteousness we seek can be categorized according to six different foundations, which he likens to "moral taste-buds": Care/Harm, Fairness/Cheating, Liberty/Oppression, Loyalty/Betrayal, Authority/Subversion, and Sanctity/Degradation. Each of these foundations appears across epochs and cultures, and where we locate ourselves on these axes will depend on both our predisposition and context. It will also serve as a pretty reliable predictor of how we vote, how we parent, what kind of a church we attend (or don't), as well as how we get along with those who differ from us.

As it relates to our current political landscape, a liberal conception of righteousness consists almost exclusively of the first three foundations (Care, Fairness, and Liberty), whereas conservative righteousness is spread across all six.

But here's the twist: most of this is unconscious, articulated not in the form of assertions but story. When asked to tell the story of their lives, liberals emphasize deep feelings about human suffering and social fairness, while conservative accounts tend to temper those same sentiments with references to respect for authority, allegiance to one's group, and purity of the self.

In terms of *Seinfeld*, Elaine's narrative about herself and the world revolves around the potential oppression and suffering an unwanted pregnancy can cause women (and children). She also appears to cherish Liberty in personal decision-making. Meanwhile, the story her boyfriend tells about the same situation, while not ignoring the factors informing Elaine's story, likely also incorporates conviction about the Sanctity of life and possibly the relevance of received wisdom (Authority). The conflict between them is not a conflict between right and wrong so much as two competing visions of right.

As the episode illustrates, and Haidt goes to great lengths to establish, divisions arise when people seek differing forms of righteousness. In fact, we may not even recognize the other's concern as righteous at all. Haidt notes, for instance, that when he speaks to liberal audiences about conservative moral foundations like Loyalty, Authority, and Sanctity, he finds that "many in the audience don't just fail to resonate; they actively reject these concerns as immoral. Loyalty to a group shrinks the moral circle; it is the basis of racism and exclusion, they say. Authority is oppression. Sanctity is religious mumbo-jumbo." You can see how automatically an us-versus-them dichotomy develops.

The diagnosis goes further. We rely on stories not just to understand the world or other people but ourselves. Depending on how tightly we hold our own stories, we can experience these divisions within. If your personal narrative involves you having long since conquered your impatience with a sibling, when you blow up at them over Thanksgiving, you'll have to rationalize or deny the eruption to keep that narrative about yourself intact.[39]

---

39. Side note: in blow-up arguments, people often develop different memories of what happened—"I never said *that*!" It's not that one person is

Religious communities are quite familiar with this phenomenon. Believers love to tell conversion stories—we call them testimonies—almost always linking spiritual belief with some form of improved behavior. Maybe we used to drink and smoke, but when we became Christians, all that changed. And it really did—for a while. But then we go through a rough patch and find ourselves hankering for a cigarette. In a moment of weakness we purchase a carton, and pretty soon we're back to a pack a day. Either we'll have to edit our testimony retroactively to let God off the hook or invest in a hefty supply of air fresheners and mints.

Whatever the case, when the reality of our life contradicts the story we have come to believe about ourselves, the development of a double life is almost a foregone conclusion. The alternative involves an intensely painful and bewildering prospect, namely, the loss of one's self-justification and the death of one's self-understanding.

We don't mean it to, but our story comes to function as a Law of Who (We Believe) We Must Be or Become, thereby preventing us from seeing reality for what it is.

The point here is not that one type of story, or set of foundations, is better than another (though they might be). The point is simply that the roots of political division tap into a wellspring as universal as it is subterranean. We are all actively identified with moral narratives that we have a large stake in being true. They are never just stories, they are *justifying* stories. Otherwise we wouldn't get so upset when those stories are threatened.

---

deliberately lying, just that each person has tweaked (subconsciously) their memories to fit the narrative they want to tell/believe. The storytelling impulse is at work all the time.

Politics as Belonging

If all that moral narratives did was divide us, then perhaps we might hold them more lightly. But shared stories bind us together as well. Part of what makes politics such an attractive replacement religion is the community it creates, the love and acceptance it offers.

I once spoke with a college student who had just finished a summer on The Hill, serving as a congressional intern. A few of his fellow interns had convinced him to delay going back to school and instead help set up an office for a gubernatorial campaign. It would be a lonely fall while the effort came together, but he'd be making a difference. Little did he know that he'd be bailing midway through to go door-to-door for a presidential nominee. The election was a long way off, but now was when the really important work began. School would still be there when the dust had settled and the country was back on track.

I'll never forget the rationale he gave me. He said, "I found *my people*," as opposed to "my purpose" or "my candidate." I had heard that phrase used to describe involvement in various subcultures— Trekkies(/ers), anarchists, boating enthusiasts, specific types of pet owners—but never a mainstream political affiliation. He had found more than solidarity. He had found belonging.

The interaction is one I've returned to often in the years since.

So fundamental is our need for connection that when belonging isn't readily found in conventional spheres like church, neighborhood, office, or home, we will look elsewhere and anywhere for it. To counteract our loneliness, we will fashion a family out of whatever resources we have at hand. It is no coincidence, then, that politics serves a *tribal* function for more and more people. Because when you share an ideological affiliation, you share not only stories and foundations but antagonisms. And nothing bonds people closer together than a common enemy.

But there's a dark side well known to anyone who has spent time in a religious community. If we are leaning on a specific cause or ideology for belonging, then those who belong *most* will be the ones who espouse their views most ardently—the louder the display, the more affirmation and admiration it will garner for the person involved. Belovedness correlates more or less directly to the strength of our commitments, indeed of our *orthodoxy.*

Belonging is thus not only conditioned on holding the right opinions or beliefs but holding them strongly enough. Soon, any hesitation becomes grounds for rejection. As *The Onion* once joked, "'We Can Have Differences of Opinion and Still Respect Each Other,' Says Betrayer of the One True Cause." And so we signal our fervor however we can, clamoring over our neighbors for the social-emotional rewards that come from being the *most* hardcore, the most purely devoted. Alas, as Stephen Marche writes in *The Unmade Bed*, "The business of correcting idealism is a parlor game in which, one by one, everybody leaves the room." Sub out "idealism" for "orthodoxy" and you're pretty close to some churches I know.

In fact, it's telling that where once we had political opinions, now we are expected to have "a politics." As in, what are *your* politics? It sounds an awful lot like what people in church mean when they talk about someone having a theology. What code dictates your life and how does it stack up to mine? They are trying to figure out whether or not you belong.

Signals Aren't Just for Turning

This word *signaling* is supremely helpful one when it comes to secu-losity of all types, especially when preceded by *virtue*. Originally coined by economists, *signaling* refers to the subtext of an action. *Virtue signaling* is simply when the subtext of an action contains an assertion of our own virtuousness. Maybe we ask a question in a public setting, not out of genuine curiosity but to indicate that we really *get it*—whatever *it* is. On the spiritual side, maybe we Insta-gram our daily devotional set-up or really go for broke in our pre-dinner prayer in order to broadcast our spiritual dedication. I know one guy who can recite the entire book of Nehemiah from memory.

Maybe we make a big deal out of liking a movie like *Black Panther* and telling everyone we know to see it not simply because we like the movie (though we may—it's great) but because we want others to know we're the type of person who likes and supports movies starring nonwhite casts. Or maybe we buy a certain type of car not only because we like the way it drives but to signal some-thing about the kind of person we are or wish to be. If I see you behind the wheel of a Prius, I know you care about the environ-ment, that you're a part of the solution, not the problem, on the side of the angels. If you drive a Ford pickup with a star-spangled license plate, I know you support American manufacturing and are proud of your roots. It doesn't mean your environmentalism or patriotism is necessarily insincere, just that the car *also* beams your ideological righteousness to those with similar stories.

I can think of no better euphemism for self-justification than *virtue signaling.*[40]

---

40. *Moral preening* might be runner-up.

Of course, just as not everyone subscribes to the seculosity of politics, not everyone signals the same thing. Perhaps we're more interested in signaling our busyness, or our success, or our intelligence, or our social class, or our enlightened nonpartisanship(!). Indeed, calling others out for virtue signaling can be a mighty convenient way not only of dismissing any public utterance we don't like but also of signaling our own superiority in the process. At the end of the day, all our signals serve the same purpose: to convince others and ourselves that we are good, right, *enough*. That we belong and are worthy of acceptance.

How unfortunate, then, that as a rule, virtue signaling backfires. Not merely because the threshold of *enough* does not exist, but because the more aggressive our signals, the less convincing we render them. What comes across instead is the extent of our insecurity—otherwise we wouldn't feel the need to preen in the first place.

Are You Washed in the Blood of the Lion?

One particularly popular, if toxic, form of virtue signaling today comes in the form of outrage. From the perspective of seculosity, public outrage functions as *the* great guilt management system of our time, especially when it comes to politics. Expressing our outrage allows us to feel like we're doing something to address the injustices we witness (and in which we're complicit)—injustices over which we often feel powerless. And who knows, maybe we are. If only rage didn't eat us alive from the inside.

I remember returning home from a trip in 2015, my travels having taken me well outside of cell-phone coverage. When I got back into range finally, I was anxious to check social media. What I found took me aback. My feeds were all consumed by shouting matches over something called "Cecil the Lion." At first, I thought I had stumbled into a Saturday Night Live skit or a viral marketing ploy of some kind.

Once I realized that the outrage was sincere, I assumed that I was missing something. At a wildlife park in Zimbabwe, an American dentist had shot and killed the beast in question. Cecil was a popular attraction, so the incident was a sad one. But why were people in my blue-state social circle two thousand miles away so upset? None of them seemed to have known about Cecil before his death. What made them so willing to yell obscenities at a complete stranger? It didn't compute.

The outcry made more sense after tracing the righteousness at work. Cecil's death triggered anyone closely identified with a moral narrative around Haidt's Care/Harm foundation. The incident told a familiar story that contained a clear villain and victim: the colonial oppressor versus the noble native. The situation was also far enough removed from everyday life that the waters wouldn't get muddied, thus making it a perfect opportunity for unleashing a cauldron of blame and condemnation.

An old Alcoholics Anonymous truism states, "The only thing better than being right is feeling wronged." Indignation can be intoxicating, especially the righteous variety. It may even be more insidious than other vices because we don't acknowledge it as pleasurable. Plus, if we have someone at whom we can point the finger and upon whom we can heap our collective guilt, maybe that will waylay us from our own daily shortcomings. Maybe if we shout loud enough about the injustice, some of the victim's righteousness will transfer to us. The human race loves a scapegoat, after all. Their blood equals our absolution.

Alas, we cannot all be equally upset—that would deny us the affirmation our anger demands. And so we start one-upping one another in search of the highest possible moral ground, clamoring for supreme indignation even when we are ostensibly on "the same team." Ideological outrage becomes a contest, in other words, where identity is at stake. Whose outrage is the most authentic? The most righteous? Whose devotion to the, er, under*cat* the most unassailable? As one commentator at the time ventured,

> Many people are drawn to defend nature and underdogs (even when they are apex predators) and to hate wealthy, lying, violent dentists. But even more than that they are drawn to feeling superior and appearing wise, and being validated accordingly.

Since the true seed of the furor had more to do with moral justification than the injustice itself, the emotions did not linger on the event long. If we rely on indignation for our validation, when new facts come to light, or when the court overturns the decision we found so unfair, our outrage has to find a new target if we are to feel like our breaths still count. Harambe perhaps?

In an age of seculosity, people are dying for meaning and, lacking any more substantive framework, will latch onto basically anything they can to get it—especially if it resonates with their preexisting sympathies—even something as outwardly inconsequential as the Cecil travesty. In fact, the absurdity of this one is why it exposes the psychology underneath so nakedly: *moral outrage fills a psychological need.* It allows a person to feel like she matters, especially when she's afraid that she doesn't.

Now, please don't misunderstand me. Given what a third-rail politics is in contemporary life, it bears repeating: to diagnose the seculosity of politics today is not to suggest that the significance of politics reduces to these dynamics. Generally speaking, the issues that drive us to the voting booth matter—for all their complexities, they really *do* have meaningful effects on the lives of individuals, of nations, of the planet. My interest lies in the ways that our political feelings, attitudes, and behaviors so often come to outstrip the problems and injustices they are ostensibly about and become tools of self-justification. Indeed, when we get religious about politics in the ways I am describing it has a way of actually undermining the significance of the issues themselves— we come to care about a thing less for itself and more because of how it makes us feel and how it affects our belonging in a given political tribe.

Politics as Meaning

Politics maintains its magnetism as a replacement religion not only because of the belonging and righteousness it promises but the meaning it provides. As stressful as shouting at people on the internet may be, the force of the convictions can also be deeply enlivening. Who doesn't want to care about something, anything, that strongly?

Essayist Jon Baskin put his finger on this dynamic when he recounted his post-college years at a partisan think-tank in Washington, DC, crafting articles that were meant to influence policy leftward. "Once you got the hang of the narratives, everything fit into them," he explained. Again, there's something consoling about the mastery these narratives provide. Like a five-point

Calvinist or a New Atheist, the mystery and confusion of life vanishes. For a spell.

Eventually, however, Baskin found the subversion of inquiry to activism tiresome and sought out a more intellectual community, working at various small progressive publications like *n+1*. He described the allure of his new environment this way:

> We were not merely going to report on progress; we were going to make it. It was exhilarating to try and live this way. It invested what might seem like trivial everyday decisions with a world-historical import.

If it sounds a bit like the soulmate myth, it's not far off. In his case, an all-encompassing political narrative proved so enticing because of the way it transformed humdrum realities into global struggles. Life took on renewed urgency and importance. Every day mattered.

But a life of comprehensive political conviction proved unsustainable. Later on, when Baskin runs out of gas, he confesses, "What it meant for everything to be in the last analysis political, I came to see, was that everything I did ought to be disciplined by my politics. But what if it wasn't? Should I then revise my politics, or myself?" If you're only supposed to like certain music, made by certain people with certain politics, what happens when you'd much rather listen to Michael Jackson and boogie down?

His description bears a strong resemblance to a classically religious dilemma, one that Christians would call *Pauline*: the tension between belief and action, a sort of friction between our personal *is* and *ought* like tectonic plates scraping up against one another. The earth will eventually quake—it's only a question of when.

Indeed, religiosity aimed mostly at living up to the *ought* of the law produces self-righteousness (if you think your behavior passes the integrity test) or burnout (if you know it doesn't). Seculosity does the same thing.

Political ideologies may saturate our lives with meaning, momentarily, but they run into a brick wall when it comes to motivation. The tenets themselves, whether they be left, right, or center, cannot endow us with the power to act wholly in accordance with them. And perhaps they're not supposed to.

No matter the system, the person caught between *is* and *ought*—between what they should do and what they actually do—eventually winds up with the same question: "Who will rescue me from this body of death?" (Romans 7:24b). This is where true religion and politics part ways.

Politics as Salvation

At the heart of the seculosity of politics lies the conviction, sometimes unspoken, that politics not only explains everything but can *fix* everything. Yet, as central and inescapable as power dynamics may be in our lives, they explain nothing completely, least of all you and me. No one can be reduced to a single set of convictions or power dynamics; to try and do so necessitates leaving something out, repressing some inner contradiction for fear of being ostracized. We effectively refuse for some part of ourselves to be known.

Put differently, there is a lot more going on in life than the political.

The feminist writer and activist Vivian Gornick once described her lifelong struggle to balance love and work along egalitarian lines. "I'd written often about living alone because I couldn't figure out why I *was* living alone," she explained. For years, her answer had to do with sexism. She blamed patriarchal men for forcing talented women like herself to choose between career and romance, a trade-off she refused on principle.

Looking back at the age of sixty-five, she admitted that her familiar explanation, while not 100 percent wrong, may have been a tad convenient. She conceded,

> Much of my loneliness was self-inflicted, having more to do with my angry, self-divided personality than with sexism. The reality was that I was alone not because of my politics, but because I did not know how to live in a decent way with another human being. In the name of equality I tormented every man who'd ever loved me until he left me; I called them on everything, never let anything go, held them up to accountability in ways that wearied us both. There was, of course, more than a grain of truth in everything I said, but those grains, no matter how numerous, need not have become the sandpile that crushed the life out of love.

This kind of honesty not only takes courage, it evinces a kind of vulnerability that's hard not to love.

Political explanations invariably involve thinking about the world in group terms. Doing so is appropriate when it comes to the distribution of resources, but it is less helpful when it comes to matters of the heart. In Gornick's case, the political explanation let her off the hook. That doesn't mean her experience of patriarchy in relationships was unfounded, only that by attributing her loneliness *exclusively* to a system, she avoided the thornier core of her predicament, and thereby pain. The truth is, her isolation had as much to do with psychology as it did oppression.

This hints at a deeper truth about politics. When Sting sang that "there is no political solution to our troubled evolution," he wasn't making an anarchist statement. Many of the problems we face in the world *can* be addressed and even solved by political means. The AIDS epidemic of the 1980s would never have been contained without government intervention. The opioid crisis currently ravaging the United States will not abate without policies regulating the use of fentanyl somehow.

The problem arises when we interpret such victories as evidence that politics is the only or even most effective path to hope, or, more ambitiously, that political action will be the means by which we achieve paradise. Would that it were so! I'm afraid, however, that W. H. Auden was onto something in his Christmas Oratorio when he wrote,

That the dream of a Perfect State or No State at all,
    To which we fly for refuge, is a part of our punishment.

An ear accustomed to the seculosity of politics might hear Auden's verse as overly defeatist or pessimistic. Yet there's nothing defeating about the truth that politics cannot save us. Far more defeating is the idea that it can but we're still waiting for the right system or leader to come along. Or it could, if only those people *over there* would get out of the way.

Politics makes an effective tool for changing people's circumstances but a considerably less effective one for changing people's minds, to say nothing of their hearts. We may be able to coerce a person to act in accordance with our vision of righteousness, but we cannot coerce them to *like* it. As anyone who's raised a child knows, rules can only take you so far in addressing the messy dynamics of human compulsion. Indeed, we run into the limits of politics when we seek political solutions to internal problems. I'm talking about hubris and lust and grief and sin and evil. *This* is the realm of trouble that Sting references in that somewhat annoying song, the layer underneath the political, what we might call the psychospiritual or the existential. This is where, despite our signals to the contrary, we actually live and dream and love and suffer.

I remember after Donald Trump was elected, those who supported Hillary Clinton complained openly and often of severe anxiety and stress. It wasn't just the run-of-the-mill "let's all move to Canada" stuff. A friend from college told me she couldn't sleep because she was so scared about what might happen. A doctor told me that his anger at the president-elect was getting in the way of his ability to treat patients.

Their reports made me feel exposed as a little superficial. I cared about what was going on, but the material occupying my emotional life, even at such a momentous time, had to do mainly with my children. I was worried about one of them in particular, but not because of who won the election. I was worried because he seemed so unhappy at school.

Fast forward a couple years, and a researcher named Seth Stephens-Davidowitz has just finished combing through mountains of Google Search data. What we search for online says a lot about what's occupying us. When we Google something, we're alone, anonymous, and unfiltered. What we enter into that search bar may not provide the whole story of our inner life, but it's certainly a decent clue.

Anyway, Stephens-Davidowitz discovered that there wasn't actually a rise in anxiety in the country after Trump was elected—not even in the most liberal areas. "When people were waking up at 3am in a cold sweat, their searches were about their job, their health, their relationship—they're not concerned about the Muslim ban or global warming."

Again, the political dimension of life remains tremendously important. But the psychospiritual dimension trumps it (!) every time. You fall in love and all of a sudden the newspaper holds very little interest. Your parent gets diagnosed with cancer, and rally, what rally? I come from a family of clergy, and of the countless deathbed visits they've made, not one person has ever wanted to talk politics. Not one! There isn't a liberal or conservative in that hospital room, just a human being.

The Only Engine of Survival

Even the best-intentioned politics leave off in the hard trenches of personal despair. But that is precisely where the balm of Christian faith begins. Because the gospel of Jesus Christ is not an improved ideology to adopt or foist on others. It is not a system but a message—one rejected by both the conservatives and liberals of his day—addressed to those who have failed to live up to their principles, about the God who meets people in their need, not their virtue. What binds its adherents together is not common righteousness but shared weakness.

There's an old joke about a pastor inviting a cynic to church. The cynic scoffs, saying, "Go to church? That den of hypocrites?" To which the pastor responds, "There's always room for one more!"

What a hopeful vision. This attitude, also known as *grace*, does not negate or invalidate our political convictions or ethical stances. Instead, it allows us to hold them more gently and more honestly. Moreover, the promise of heaven relieves us of the burden of fixing the world single-handedly, a burden that was never ours in the first place. It puts our fractious political arrangements in a proper light—the light of eternity.

Far from discouraging acts of love, such a perspective tends to do the opposite. Grace permits us to see both others and ourselves as we are: flawed people who do not have all the answers—and who should be suspicious of those who seem to think they do. We are much more likely to work to improve our neighbors' welfare when we no longer see them as an obstacle to utopia. When we see them, instead, as a lot like us, desperate to belong but caught up in narratives that divide them from others and themselves.

Toward the end of the book of Luke, Jesus points to the temple in Jerusalem, the nucleus of Jewish religious and political life, and says something remarkable. "As for these things that you see, the days will come when not one stone will be left upon another; all will be thrown down" (Luke 21:6). If he was trying to coin a catchy campaign slogan, he failed.

To those who would absolutize systems of government and the power dynamics inherent to them, Christ underlines their impermanence. All that we see—every headline, every scandal, everything that seems so pressing at the moment, the legislative, judicial, and executive branch—none of it will last. Maybe that scares you, or maybe that gives you hope. Either way, his message doesn't end there. In the same passage, Jesus assures his followers that despite the tumult surrounding them, "not a hair of your head will perish" (Luke 21:18).

Some believe that it was Jesus himself who got the ball rolling on the destruction of the temple. When he died, the Bible tells us, the ceremonial curtain that separated the presence of God and his people was torn in two, dismantling the divide between sinful humanity and a holy God.

This is the Jesus who can't ever be definitively politicized, the one who relinquished his rightful power for the sake of those whose outrage put him on a cross. His only signal back is love to the loveless shown.

In other words, not the messiah we would elect but the one who elects *us*.

CHAPTER 9

THE SECULOSITY
OF JESUSLAND

It takes guts to switch careers under any circumstances. But it takes extra guts when the career you're leaving is something as highly esteemed as teaching. You can't really blame the money, since no one goes into it to get rich. You can't blame the sacrifice, since that would be superficial. And you can't blame the students, because that would be callous.

Those who take on the mantle of teacher usually see it as a vocation, even a calling, and for good reason—it's really hard and undeniably virtuous. Which means that when you bail, you haven't just opted out of a specific way of making a living but on a full-blooded purpose, maybe even how you see yourself. It feels—and certainly appears to others—like a moral defeat.

So when my friend Alex told me he was quitting his job as an elementary-school teacher, I could safely assume he had already received more than enough judgment from others and himself. I needed to tread lightly.

His reasoning surprised me. It wasn't the long hours or short pay or even the red tape. He had not lost his love for the kids, nor had he stopped believing that he could make a difference in their lives. He hadn't even been discouraged by the cycles of poverty that many of his students' families were trapped in.

His beef was with what he called "the pathology of transformation" that had infiltrated the profession—in his context at least. The way Alex saw it, the emphasis on getting the kids to where they *should* be prevented teachers from meeting kids where they actually *were*. He confessed that he had begun viewing his students almost exclusively in terms of the test scores upon which his job depended, metrics that, truth be told, were not indicating overwhelming amounts of achievement.

Reading between the lines, it sounded like Alex had begun to lose sight of these kids as people and had slowly begun to resent them for not doing more, wanting more, being more.

Kids being kids, they picked up on his attitude, and as the feeling in the classroom soured, so did the test scores. One day, after writing up a third-grader whose parent had died two weeks previous, he realized that unless he took a hiatus and got some perspective, he would head down a bitter road.

I'm no expert on pedagogy, but I do know that a teacher's job is to educate. They are paid to help students learn and grow and think, to bring their pupils from point A to point B on the knowledge chart. Without tests to measure the progress, what did an instructor have to go on? If Alex was so hung up on evaluation, perhaps he had gone into the wrong profession after all.

The punchline here is that he was considering going into Christian ministry. I asked him why he was so sure he wouldn't find the same "pathology of transformation" in the church. I regretted the question before it came out of my mouth. There's a time and place for healthy skepticism, and this was not it. He gave me the kind of look that said, "Gee, Dave, thanks a *lot*."

My response may have been cheeky, but the underlying reality is anything but. The same performancism and cult of productivity that dogs other areas of modern life dogs the church.

The Law of Jesusland

There have always been competing visions of the Christian church. Long before the days of shopfront congregations and long before the Protestant Reformation, Christians disagreed, profoundly, on what a church should look like, how it should function, who it is meant to serve. The letters collected in the New Testament address church bodies that look quite disparate.

One of the more common areas of disagreement boils down to a single question: is the church a hospital for sinners or a schoolhouse for saints? Or, put in more contemporary language, does it prioritize relief or growth?

On paper, this might sound like a false dichotomy. Instead of positioning the two aims as mutually exclusive or in competition, the church should simply pursue both avenues. It should be a place for the wounded to find healing *and* the healthy to be trained in providing that healing. If only the situation were that clear-cut.

But wait a second. If seculosity refers to religious energy directed at secular or horizontal targets, why talk about church? You would presume that Religion is exempt from our diagnosis.

The tragic irony of Jesusland—a not-altogether-flattering catchall for the bastardized form of Protestant Christianity that dominates much of the spiritual landscape in the West—is that it often resembles its secular replacements more than the Real Thing. I'm not sure if the former has influenced the latter, or vice versa, but the similarities between our small-r religions and what remains of the capital-R variety are uncanny.

You may have noticed that the strands of seculosity we've explored thus far all operate more or less identically. They cast a vision of enoughness and then implore us to realize that vision with forbearance, grit, and hard currency, for the sake of existential reward. If you eat well enough, love well enough, parent well enough, stay busy enough, you will *be* enough. This is the promise at the heart of what we might call *a religion of law*, and it applies to every replacement religion under the sun.

The word *law* is a broad one. A law spells out both how we should behave and what will happen to us if we don't. As such, a law is a conditional proposition: not just do this or don't do that, but *if* you do X, Y, or Z sensible thing, *then* you will be considered a good citizen. If you don't, well, that makes you a criminal. The law classifies and categorizes. It tells us clearly and confidently where we stand. Taken together, our laws comprise a vision of righteousness that cannot be divorced from the values that shape it.

A capital-R Religion of law bestows divine favor on those who conform to its conception of righteousness, a.k.a. those who act in accordance with the Thou Shalt's and Thou Shalt Not's that God has laid out.

A small-r religion of law promises functional salvation to those who live up to its demands, expressed more often than not in the *should's* and *ought's* we infer from our shared ideals. Thou Ought to be Skinny or Influential or Effortlessly Sophisticated, and so on, if you want to be accepted, respected, or admired.

There's a fundamental problem with all religions of law, in whatever form we encounter them. The problem does not reside in the content of the law itself. The problem resides in the human heart: knowing what we should do or be does not give us the ability to do or be those things. Not when it really comes down to it.

For example, a friend sees that I'm stressed out over something minor and tells me, "just relax." I may acknowledge the wisdom of her advice, I may wish with all my might that I could just relax, but the furrow in my brow won't unlock. If anything, I start worrying about how I'm coming across to my friends.

The law never has and never will inspire what it commands, at least not in any comprehensive or lasting sense. Sometimes we think that if we just trumpet the law more loudly, or cloak it in words of affection, it will do the trick and change our loved one's behavior (or our own). Alas, looking to instruction to change a person, deep down, amounts to a fool's errand when it comes to a species that Aldous Huxley once characterized as "the pillars, but . . . also the dynamite; simultaneously the beams and the dry rot." What he meant was the same thing William Faulkner did when he famously invited would-be authors to return to the only source of good writing, which is "the human heart in conflict with itself."

As unpopular as it may be to admit, each of us experiences division within ourselves, some tension between Should and Want. To invoke *Seinfeld* once more, no one is fully "master of their domain." Even when we know what goodness and righteousness look like, we rebel. "I do not understand my own actions. For I do not do what I want, but I do the very thing I hate," writes the apostle Paul in the seventh chapter of Romans, articulating what philosopher Hannah Arendt calls his most towering discovery. I'm reminded of a favorite piece of graffiti: on the side of a building, someone has spray-painted "Spread Anarchy." A second artist has crossed out the slogan, writing above it, "Don't tell me what to do!"

Religions of law may succeed in the short term because they appeal to our yearning for control, but they run out of steam eventually when confronted with the realities of human conflictedness.

Furthermore, as anyone who has tried to hang their self-regard on a target of seculosity finds out, *enough* turns out to be a mirage, ever retreating into the distance. Just ask Markus Persson, the mind behind the viral video-game craze *Minecraft*. Shortly after selling his company for billions of dollars and getting what he calls "everything," he tweeted to the world that he was "hanging out in Ibiza with a bunch of friends and partying with famous people, able to do whatever I want, and I've never felt more isolated." Entrepreneurial dynamo Elon Musk has expressed a similar despondency. Lady Gaga as well. The list goes on.

Religions of law promise wholeness and peace, but as the preceding chapters illustrate, they ultimately deliver anxiety, self-consciousness, and loneliness. A culture awash in seculosity is therefore a culture of despair.

A Deeper Magic

Christianity purports something different. It tells of a God who is not shy about handing down law. The Ten Commandments outline just such a code of behavior, and in the Sermon on the Mount, Jesus doubles down on its injunctions, claiming that the Thou Shalt's delivered to the Israelites by Moses apply to human motivation as well as behavior. It's not just that we shouldn't commit murder, he tells us, we shouldn't even *think* about it. The same holds true for adultery and avarice. The law found in Scripture is *tough*, so tough that the only reasonable response to taking it seriously is desperation.

Yet Jesus does not end there. After the Law has robbed his hearers of any chance of achieving divinely appointed enoughness on their own, he hints at the possibility of what C. S. Lewis called "a deeper magic." Jesus says that what's impossible with humans is possible with God.

We may not be able to answer the question of our own not-enoughness, but that doesn't mean there isn't an answer.

It's one thing to say such things, and another to embody them. In his death, Christians believe, Jesus suffered the full weight of human sin and by his resurrection he extends pardon, righteousness, and eternal life—even to those who put him there. The cross declares that the guilt and shame we spend our days trying in vain to expiate via sweat and scapegoating is absolved, past, present, and future.

To put this in a less conventionally religious way: it is no accident that the core of the Jesus story dovetails so well with the human dilemma of not-enoughness that propels our seculosity. If so much of our energy—and so much of our suffering—is caught up in the quest for justification, it should not be surprising that this same dilemma finds a direct response in the central thrust of the Christian religion.

No doubt this heat-seeking forgiveness accounts for the magnetism of Christianity in prisons. The too-good-to-be-true message of mercy, grounded in history and hemoglobin as opposed to sentiment or theory, speaks directly to criminals and failures, and all those bowed down by life's crushing load. As one of my mentors used to say, grace moves beyond deserving. It is the hope of the hopeless and the final word on God's disposition toward troubled people like you and me. I'm simplifying things, but not by much.

Christianity at its core is a religion of law *and* grace, which is to say, *a religion of grace*, since grace has no meaning apart from law. The upright have no need of clemency, the healthy no need of a doctor, the righteous no need of a savior.

The seculosity of Jesusland takes root when law supplants grace as Christianity's final word. Or when we subvert the immortal hymn with our additions: "I once was lost but now am found, so I better stay found!" We start asking ourselves, if Jesus caught and embraced me when I fell off the ladder of life, then why does it feel like I'm on a new ladder now? Why do I get the creeping suspicion that I'm not a good enough *Christian*? The seculosity of Jesusland seeps in when church turns into yet another venue to establish our enoughness, rather than the only reliable place to receive it.

More Than Meets the Eye

One of the chief ways Christianity morphs into seculosity occurs under the heading *transformation*. As exciting a prospect as transformation may be, when it takes center stage in a person's spiritual life, it swallows up grace and turns Christianity into a vehicle of anxiety and exhaustion.

Conservative or traditionally minded Christians tend to talk about transformation in personal terms, whereas more progressive Christians usually frame transformation systemically or collectively. But whether the goal is personal holiness or social progress, the same dynamic holds sway: faith serves as a means to an end, a spiritual method of producing such-and-such result.

Take the more conservative end of the spectrum. American Evangelicalism gets a bad rap. And considered as movement, American Evangelicalism often deserves its reputation as a neurosis-inducing, moralistic, anti-intellectual purveyor of bad movies—and worse music. At its worst, it bears only a passing resemblance to its namesake (*evangelical* meaning *good-news centered*). But like anyone, actual Evangelicals rarely fit that mold. Spend time at a megachurch, and you'll encounter radical humility and generosity just as often as the caricatured rigidity. At the risk of heresy, I don't find Baptists to be significantly more judgmental than any other groups of humans.

And yet, in its emphasis on personal transformation, American Evangelicalism often seems more American than Evangelical. I've run into too many former, or "recovering," Evangelicals to discount the deep-seated and oppressive performancism at work, where what matters more than what God has done for you is what you can and need to do for God. This usually boils down to a set of prohibitions that expire when you get married (or turn twenty-one), tempered by well-meaning injunctions about service, generosity, and evangelism. Church, in this vein, very much functions as a schoolhouse for saints, its principal purpose being to produce holiness and even happiness in the present lives of its members.

This sort of spiritual performancism runs on fuel very similar to that which powers the seculosity of politics. To get a handle on the vicissitudes of the world, we craft a story about our life and tell it to both others and ourselves. In this case, we call it our testimony, and its trajectory is by definition upward. "I used to be (unhappy, selfish, addicted, mean, lonely, fill in the blank), then I met Jesus, and now I'm (happy, generous, healthy, responsible, kind, etc.)."

You can hardly fault a person for wanting to celebrate what he feels God has done in his life. Spend enough time in a community of Christians, and you will meet people who *have* been delivered from all manner of adversity. These things happen, and they're wonderful.

But when faith is tied too tightly to changes in behavior, it is put at odds (and in competition) with other "spiritual products" and the results they yield. Christianity itself starts to resemble a self-improvement scheme on spiritual steroids, only as reliable as the personal growth it may have produced, which we know—from both experience and Scripture—is not always that reliable.

Say you had an honest-to-God conversion experience in your twenties. Things legitimately get better in your life. Maybe hope blooms in your heart for the first time in ages, or you take yourself a little less seriously. Maybe you rediscover the moral compass you thought you'd lost for good. But then your forties roll around and certain besetting problems persist. You may be a bit quicker to admit when you're wrong about something, but you're just as prone to anxiety and self-loathing as you ever have been. Some circumstances even appear to get worse.

For the gospel to retain its power, you'll either have to edit your testimony or hide the things that contradict your story. Otherwise you'd have to interpret each regression as evidence of God's absence or disdain, both prospects equally terrifying. Pretty soon you are living in a spiritualized version of that *New Yorker* cartoon of the man holding his companion's hand, telling her, "I can't promise I'll change, but I promise I'll *pretend* to change."

The dissonance between who we feel we're supposed to be (as New Creations) and who we actually are hurts and can prompt the cruelest kinds of rationalizations. On a larger scale, this kind of theology creates an environment of suspicion and blame, where otherwise kind people start monitoring one another's devotion, keeping score at every opportunity, usually for the sake of propping up their own. What once was joyful devolves into something joyless, a driver of added exhaustion rather than a respite from it, the very opposite of Christ's timeless invitation, "Come to me, all you that are weary and carrying heavy burdens, and I will give you rest" (Matthew 11:28). You can understand why more and more people would elect to sleep in on Sunday.

To put the situation in theological terms, a gospel based on personal sanctification is no gospel at all. It produces refugees.

The Other End of the Telescope

Ironically enough—I've seen this time after time after time—those refugees often flee to what they perceive to be the opposite of the oppressively individualistic and often hypocritical moralism that burned them out: an outwardly liberal expression of Christianity that emphasizes social transformation over personal holiness.

It's true: the main other way that Christianity moves from a religion of grace into one of law happens under progressive auspices. Perhaps in reaction to the louder and larger conservative branch of the faith, believers trade one set of imperatives for another, shifting their focus to systemic morality. Instead of sermons on the ills of sexual promiscuity or greed, preachers target racial prejudice, xenophobia, and the excesses of capitalism.

Thus, mainline Christians on social media start saying things like, "if your church doesn't preach about immigration reform this Sunday, it's time to go to another church," the implication being that a church is called first and foremost to stand with the downtrodden against the powerful, a servant to the servants, a prophetic witness against the forces of hate and bigotry. Which is hardly outside of its brief, historically speaking. The Bible has as much to say about feeding the poor and welcoming the outcast as it does about chastity and prayer, if not more.

While beautiful in theory, however, the church in these cases is left with little to say to the perpetrators themselves, the *sinners* in the equation. Forgiveness, if offered to such villains at all, only comes after protracted displays of self-flagellation. It has to be *earned*. Acceptance into the community of saints quietly depends on assent to common convictions on right versus wrong, rather than an admission of common hypocrisy and shared need for mercy—or faith in who the Book of Common Prayer calls the One "whose property is always to have mercy."[41] Church members still police one another's doctrine, it's just the content of that doctrine that's shifted. Admittedly, with eternal stakes out the window (or simply ignored), the tone often softens. But stick around long enough and the question comes up: are you doing *enough* to bear witness to God's love of "the least of these"?

The church in this iteration remains just as much a schoolhouse for saints as ever, not a place predominantly of comfort but of *challenge*. The basic aim and method of this branch does not differ from those in its conservative counterparts: tell the people in the pew what they need to do so that they'll go out there and do it. In other words, perform dammit!

Alas, the flaw in the heart doesn't vary along political lines. Paul's discovery that "I do not do the good I want, but the evil I do not want is what I do" crosses every aisle. Which means that if social transformation forms the heart of the preaching you either give or receive, resentment is a foregone conclusion, just as

---

41. My favorite euphemism for what the church is called to be comes from author Francis Spufford, who calls it "the league of the guilty."

it is when personal sanctification makes for the primary message. Instead of loving your neighbor, you start to hate her for not evincing compassion, or not evincing *enough* compassion. Yourself too.

Once faith and social justice become interchangeable, though, a funny thing often happens. Dutiful activists realize that the church isn't all that efficient a purveyor of progress. I'm not referring solely to the bureaucracy or institutional inertia or even the reputation. No, the God stuff seems to get in the way. Maybe it creeps potential allies out, or maybe it distracts our comrades from the important work in front of them. Whatever the case, it's a fairly short step off the broad church train to more overt forms of seculosity.

Inconveniently, however, the law always follows us into the station of secular do-gooding. In a trenchant essay titled "Excommunicate Me from the Church of Social Justice," activist Frances Lee draws the parallels between the two communities adroitly:

> When I was a Christian, all I could think about was being good, showing goodness, and proving to my parents and my spiritual leaders that I was on the right path to God. All the while, I believed I would never be good enough, so I had to strain for the rest of my life towards an impossible destination of perfection.
>
> I feel compelled to do the same things as an activist a decade later. I self-police what I say in activist spaces. I stopped commenting on social media with questions or pushback on leftist opinions for fear of being called out. I am always ready to apologize for anything I do that a community member deems wrong, oppressive, or inappropriate—no questions asked. The amount of energy I spend demonstrating purity

in order to stay in the good graces of fast-moving activist community is enormous.

What binds both expressions of Jesusland together, and makes them such close cousins of seculosity, is their scope as much as their scorekeeping. Both forms restrict God's purposes so entirely to the here-and-now that they render any longer view incomprehensible. Christianity is a means to an earthly end, almost a way of *using* God to fix the world or yourself. To borrow a fancy phrase, Jesusland Christianity operates squarely within "the immanent frame," removed from the transcendent realities that have defined the faith throughout the millennia. Eventually, one starts to wonder if our near-myopic focus on *this* life masks a faltering confidence in the one to come.

Whatever the case, life both in- and outside of Jesusland is no longer a vale of tears to be endured until the long-awaited, twinkling-of-an-eye transformation, so much as a game to be won (which everyone loses). In practice, this is the difference between being surprised by moments of joy—and personal growth—versus expecting them.

Come Thou Long Expected Disclaimer

Criticizing *transformation* is a dodgy business. It usually comes across as a poo-pooing of hope. It can also signal a tentativeness about God's presence in our lives or a reluctance to ascribe any real power to the Holy Spirit.[42]

----

42. For all its blatant materialism, one area where the "prosperity gospel" shines is in its insistence that God is not a concept or set of theological assertions but an active force in the world—and in our actual lives—for good.

Yet as with every other area we've surveyed, the point here is not that transformation is somehow bad. I would be tempted to label that person a sociopath who could look at themselves and their surroundings with any degree of attentiveness or honesty without desiring transformation. Life is hard. The world is a rough place. Yearning for peace and holiness among all nations— for the kingdom of God—constitutes the height of goodness. To imply otherwise would be antithetical to Christianity. It would be nihilism.

The issue does not lie with the possibility of transformation but the *guarantee* of transformation. Not because transformation is painful or difficult, but because the guarantee often precludes the possibility. As my friend Alex learned firsthand, the more pressure he put on his students to improve, the worse they performed. The more they *had* to transform—for the sake of the school's funding or Alex's flagging self-regard—the more resistance they experienced to doing so. It's hard to teach a person something when you're mad at them for not already knowing it or when you're constantly interrupting the learning process to make measurements. The motivation on both sides simply dries up.

Fortunately for Alex, third-graders aren't very good at pretending. Feigning personal improvement for the sake of approval is a skill we learn over time.

When we impose religious standards of enoughness on adults, in lieu of actual spiritual transformation—which is usually unconscious and apparent to our friends before it is to us—we delude others and ourselves, all the while getting more and more stuck

---

That, I'd wager, is why Pentecostal Christianity continues to explode around the world as other expressions decline. It's not a head-trip. Suffering people don't want ideas about God, they want God, full stop.

in a morbid cycle of moral pulse-taking. Sadly, no plant can grow if it's being dug up every five minutes to monitor its growth. A watched pot and all that.

Christianity loses its animating potency when positioned first and foremost as a means to personal or collective transformation. "Thou shalt transform" becomes the imperative du jour, no different in impact from the edicts we receive via every other area of seculosity—anxiety, narcissism, loneliness, and despair. This does not mean that Christians are somehow prohibited from valuing or seeking after progress, just that genuine transformation is the fruit of grace, not its precondition. Put in nonreligious terms, people only truly change when they no longer feel they have to in order to be loved.

What makes Christianity a religion of grace, ultimately, is its essential revelation: of a God who meets us in both our individual *and* collective sin with a love that knows no bounds, the kind of love that lays down its life for its enemies. It is not a roadmap to engineering spiritual enoughness but the glorious proclamation that on account of Christ, you and I *are* enough—right now, right here, before we do or say anything. That is to say, Christianity at its sustaining core is not a religion of good people getting better, but of *real* people coping with their failure to be good.

It Came from the Basement

No matter what religion of law, guilt-management system, or arbiter of enoughness we pledge our devotion to, the frailty and finitude of our condition as human beings—our abiding sinfulness— ensures that we will all come up short eventually. We may be able to maintain our performance, or the appearance of performance, for a while. But sooner or later, everyone hits up against the hard limits of their DNA. Punk or prep, mod or rocker, life makes a failure out of all of us. No one ultimately escapes the tragic dimension of the human condition.[43]

Failure is where religions of law crumble, the place where our guilt proves unmanageable, the turning point that marks the point-of-no-return, justification-wise. There's nothing more useless (or sad) than a schoolhouse for saints when everyone has flunked out.

The situation sounds dire, and in a lot of ways it is. Just not where a religion of grace is concerned. This is because a religion of grace *begins* with failure.

Take, for example, what may be the preeminent hospital for sinners around, Alcoholics Anonymous. There is something arresting about the fact that the refugees and casualties of Jesusland need look no further for light and healing than the basements of the very institutions that have quickened their demise. After all, the only requirement for entry into the recovery meetings hosted one floor down from so many a church sanctuary is an admission of failure.

Steps one and two of the Twelve Steps make this feature plain: "We admitted we were powerless over alcohol—that our lives had become unmanageable. We came to believe that a Power greater than ourselves could restore us to sanity." Sub out "alcohol" for *sin* or *life* or *ourselves* and you have a one-way ticket out of Jesusland.

---

43. Perhaps this is part of why senior citizens gravitate toward church the way they do. Experience (translation: failure) opens them up to the message of the cross—a message that takes into account the storms and shipwrecks of life—in ways that no amount of exhortation could. After all, transformation simply does not have the same appeal to a seventy-year-old as a thirty-year-old. Mercy on the other hand . . .

In AA there are notably no clergy or leaders of any kind, only volunteers who wield no more power than the newest member of the group. No doctors walk the halls of this hospital other than the Great Physician. This means that it will never be a place for celebrity pastors who buy into their own hype. It will never attract fearful bureaucrats looking to justify their desire for control over others. The anonymity ensures that opportunities for glory—for example, being an outstanding sponsor—will be supremely limited. There's no authority to abuse.

But it also means that AA lacks any ladder or hierarchy for its members to climb, or pretend to climb. Even if there were, those in attendance usually have far too many skeletons in their closets and misdemeanors on their resumés to maintain any pretense of justification. In fact, no one present is expected to be anything other than a complete and utter mess—otherwise they wouldn't be there. Those who attempt to boast of their sobriety are roundly and publicly shot down. You do far worse in AA to deny your weakness than to acknowledge it. As one member of AA puts it,

> Imagine walking into a church where all who entered were asked to sign a waiver at the door that said: "I'm a sinner and by stepping into the room today I acknowledge that fact." Ministry and church life would be tremendously more effective. Unfortunately, you can come into church these days and sign up for any number of identities: Easter/Christmas type, fanatic/Pharisee, sinner, middle-of-the-road, or whatever. In AA, there is only the option of sinner.

Any time a person speaks at an AA meeting, they are obliged to introduce themselves by saying, "Hi, I'm Alice and I'm an alcoholic." That goes for the first-time visitor as well as the person who's been there for forty years. This often-caricatured practice undercuts any false confidence in the alcoholic's own strength or track record. For this reason, members have been known to say that the person who's been sober the longest at any given meeting is the person who woke up first that day. That is, once an alcoholic, never *not* an alcoholic. Sobriety, a.k.a. survival, is the object here—not transformation.

As a result, the "theology" of AA, such as it is, does not dwell on secondary questions. God is who you need to save you—without whose intervention you will die—and the rest is just window-dressing. Oddly enough, this emphasis on personal salvation above all else creates a community of mutual service and sacrifice that puts most churches to shame, perhaps because it flows out of shared weakness—*persistent* shared weakness—rather than any shared strength. Humility is both the beginning and end.

Furthermore, since AA deals in survival rather than progress, its members exhibit virtually no insecurity when confronted with other spiritual products, including atheism. They don't get drawn into tiresome arguments with skeptics. After all, arguments frequently served as ammunition to enable their drinking. Their own continued existence is the only proof they need for their program and the Higher Power upon which it depends. Without divine intervention, they know for certain that they'd be dead. Others can believe whatever they'd like—it changes nothing. "Technically Christians need their own program just as desperately," writer Helen Andrews observes, "but for some reason they're still more likely to get defensive about it."

I find the entire phenomenon tremendously hopeful. After all, AA started in 1939 with two drunks, and today has more members than Chicago has residents. Its growth has been explosive, not the fruit of some well-oiled publicity campaign but of hundreds of thousands of left-for-dead addicts claiming that God has done for them what they could not do for themselves.

Would that the refugees of Jesusland and the burnouts of seculosity more generally—by which I mean all of us—might stumble on something like a Sinners Anonymous. Lord knows we wouldn't have to look far. I have it on good authority that, obscured as they may be, the seeds can be found on the ground floor of the church building, among those foolish enough to claim that the God who saves hopeless cases and repeat offenders has a name.

No, not Bill W. (or Jesus C.). I'm thinking of Luella Bates Washington Jones.

Thank You, M'am

In 1958, the great American poet and playwright Langston Hughes published a (very) short story that traces the shape of grace with astounding clarity and richness, "Thank You, M'am." There are only two characters in the story, a boy named Roger and a "large woman with a large purse" named Luella Bates Washington Jones. Luella is walking home alone late at night when Roger runs up and tries to steal her purse. Before he can get away, Luella grabs the boy and won't let him go. He's in for it, we think. She seems like the kind of lady people used to refer to as a "battle-ax."

Luella asks Roger why he tried to snatch her bag, and after telling a couple lies—which she calls him on—he comes clean: he wanted money to buy a pair of blue suede shoes. Hughes wants to unburden us of our sympathy for this boy. Roger wasn't acting out of hunger or desperation—he was acting out of greed.

Roger assumes that Luella's getting ready to haul him into jail, but instead she brings him home with her, washes his face, and tells him that she knows what it's like to want things you can't get. Then, in lieu of a lecture, Luella cooks him a meal, complete with dessert.

Her unexpected behavior has a strange effect on Roger. When they entered her apartment, Luella had laid her purse on the day-bed where he could easily grab it and bolt. But curiously enough, he finds that he no longer wants to. Instead, he hears himself ask Luella if she needs someone to go to the store to get her milk. She demurs, filling his plate again:

> The woman did not ask the boy anything about where he lived, or his folks, or anything else that would embarrass him. Instead, as they ate, she told him about her job in a hotel beauty shop that stayed open late, what the work was like, and how all kinds of women came in and out, blondes, red-heads, and Spanish. Then she cut him a half of her ten-cent cake.
>
> "Eat some more, son," she said.
>
> When they were finished eating, she got up and said, "Now here, take this ten dollars and buy yourself some blue suede shoes." . . .
>
> She led him down the hall to the front door and opened it. "Good night! Behave yourself, boy!" she said, looking out into the street as he went down the steps.

The boy wanted to say something else other than, "Thank you, m'am," to Mrs. Luella Bates Washington Jones, but although his lips moved, he couldn't even say that as he turned at the foot of the barren stoop and looked up at the large woman in the door. Then she shut the door.

What Roger receives from Luella is the opposite of what he deserved. He broke the law in no uncertain terms, yet Luella responds with warmth, welcome, and even reward. Her reaction lies so far outside the logic of this-for-that as to be absurd. Isn't she afraid of being taken advantage of, we wonder? What about consequences? Aren't her actions irresponsible?

Luella doesn't ignore Roger's transgression or shrug it off. Nor does she punish him, as she would have every right to do. Because she sees herself in the boy, the intervention she offers goes beyond mere restraint, reaching into the depths of motivation. The counterintuitive treatment he experiences inspires a change of heart in the boy. Sitting there in her apartment, he no longer *wants* to do wrong. Luella bears the cost of Roger's misdeed, financial as well as relational, and it makes all the difference.

In a few short pages, Hughes paints an indelible picture of something other than retribution. He captures, in narrative form, the only force with the power to inspire what the laws of control and enoughness command, the kind of love that succeeds where judgment fails, the deeper magic of grace.

Take note: good behavior does not bring Roger into contact with Mrs. Luella Bates Washington Jones, and it won't bring us there either. Only bad behavior does the trick. Poor performance, not flying colors. Failure. Which is good news for those among us whose scores on the test of life keep getting worse—even those of us who keep getting ensnared by the false promise of seculosity, despite knowing better.

Glimpsed through the lens of a cross, what looks like the end may be only the beginning. The birth pangs of a new pathology, one of mercy—for failed teachers and their flailing students, lonely pastors and their exhausted congregants, addicts and their enablers, Christians and non-Christians, you and me.

CONCLUSION:
WHAT TO "DO" ABOUT IT

've strung us along far enough. Time to stop playing and fess up. The subtitle under which we've been working is misleading. Sorry. "What to *do* about seculosity?" By this point, it should be clear that the abundance of *doing*—whether that be performing, producing, earning, climbing, or proving—is a big part of what's making life in the twenty-first century so tough.

We can scarcely conceive of ourselves anymore apart from our *doing*, or what Christians call *works*. We construct ladders out of whatever materials we have at hand, shoddy or not, and erect scoreboards where they don't belong. We chase our enoughness into every corner of our lives, driving everyone around us—and ourselves—crazy. Self-justification may not be the only thing going on in life, but it occupies a much larger slice of our day-to-day existence than most of us would care to acknowledge.

Again, our religious crisis today is not that religion is on the wane, but that we are more religious than ever, and about too many things. We are almost never *not* in church.

This past summer, the lesson-we-never-learn slapped me in the face again. My family and I had just arrived at the beach. We had been cooped up in a car all day, counting the seconds until we'd feel the sand under our toes. My oldest son in particular was chomping at the bit. The beach, you see, is his favorite place on earth.

Which is why my heart sank like a stone when I spied the sign on the lifeguard tower: "Caution: Riptide."

I knew my only recourse would be to tell a story that had taken on an almost mythic status in our family: The Time Your Grandfather Got Caught in a Riptide and Almost Died.

It happened when my wife was young. One summer, during their annual beach pilgrimage, an unseen current swept her father out to sea without any warning. It was a clear day, he was an experienced swimmer, but that didn't matter. One second he was in view, enjoying the surf, the next he was receding toward the horizon, his wife and daughters frantically shouting his name. He survived, thank God, but the experience traumatized everyone who witnessed it.

I don't know exactly what causes a riptide. Friends have tried to explain it to me numerous times, but the details remain fuzzy, something about rising water and uneven levels of beach. What I do know is that you don't want to get stuck in one. And you *definitely* don't want one of your kids to. Shark attacks may get all the press, but riptides actually pose the bigger threat to beachgoers today. They account for about a hundred deaths every year along the US coastline. And the reason people drown is that they panic and swim against the current, toward the shore. The force of the water not only exhausts their energy, it drags them under. The whole thing is very scary.

While I may not be sure of what causes a riptide, or even how to spot one, my wife has made damn sure I know how to survive one. The key, it turns out, is not to resist but "go with the flow." No joke. Instead of exerting yourself, allow the current to take you out to sea. The tidal forces will settle after a minute or two and dump you in safer spot.

Your life depends on letting go of control.

A similar dynamic applies to the seculosity in which we are currently drowning. Our attempts to engineer our own salvation backfire, and do so dramatically. When our initial strokes get us nowhere, instead of reevaluating or giving up, we start paddling in a different direction, with the same results.[44] I hate to say it, but the only life raft capable of reaching a world drowning in seculosity will not be inflated with anything we do or don't do, but what God himself has done and is doing.

I often wish this were not the case. Part of me hopes that something suitable floats out there in the ether, just around the corner, and we simply haven't found it yet. What a relief it would be to find a foothold of meaning and enoughness that doesn't involve surrender, some genuine-article balm for our anxiety that would assuage "the strange persistence of guilt," free of the baggage and hurt that so often accompanies the faith of Abraham, Isaac, and Joseph.

I'm afraid Walker Percy had it right, though. The great Southern writer who brought us novels like *The Moviegoer* and unclassifiable delights like *Lost in the Cosmos* once published a self-interview of "Questions They Never Asked Me." After confirming—to himself—that he does indeed believe in the teachings of the church, he pressed the point. "How is such a belief possible in this day and age?" Percy asked himself.

---

44. Seculosity has become such a force of nature that it can hardly be contained in nine chapters. Once you put on the glasses, it's the sort of thing you see everywhere. A few other topics I was tempted to explore were the seculosity of celebrity, the seculosity of sports, and the seculosity of happiness. Scientism was on the list too.

His answer is my own: "What else is there?"

A few exchanges later Percy makes his meaning clear:

> This life is too much trouble, far too strange, to arrive at the end of it and then to be asked what you make of it and have to answer "Scientific humanism." That won't do. A poor show. Life is a mystery, love is a delight. Therefore I take it as axiomatic that one should settle for nothing less than the infinite mystery and the infinite delight, i.e., God.

Diverting as some of our replacement religions may be (food!), they turn to dust under the burden of human suffering, contradiction, and need. In the light of sin and death, they look not just damaging but, well, incredibly lame.

And yet, the old capital-R Religions could be just as infused with moralism—which probably has quite a bit to do with their decline. The same will no doubt happen with these new ones. The damage will catch up. It always does.

Clearly, the alternative to our initially appealing but ultimately oppressive small-r religions is not some fresh religion of law, or the (wholly theoretical) absence of religion. Our best bet would be a religion of grace—not another direction among many, but what happens when the swimming stops.

Too bad religions of grace don't grow on trees. I wish they did! If you find one, hold tight to it. There are secular expressions that do a decent job of approximating some of the deeper magic, and I thank God for them. A good therapist, for example, serves as an unconditional ally to their patient, providing the refuge from expectation and judgment we need in order to process our pain.

Of course, for the arrangement to work, you have to forget you're *paying* the therapist to provide this service.[45] Because if you know you've paid them, the love and space they extend will only go so far toward soothing your loneliness and hurt. This is similar to dreaming up a gracious God for ourselves. If I dream him up, I don't *feel* very loved. And I certainly don't trust whatever forgiveness that deity may extend.

Crafting a religion of grace from scratch may be better than nothing, but it's ultimately a self-defeating enterprise. For love and mercy to penetrate our hearts, they must be true, or at least perceived as such. A religion of grace must be *received* rather than constructed. The gifts we give ourselves don't hold a candle to the ones that truly come from an outside party, especially the ones that come by surprise.

This is why the historical element of Christianity—that Jesus lived and died and rose again—isn't arbitrary but essential. Without the visceral yet well-attested events of Christ's passion, the announcement that "we have been justified through faith, [and therefore] we have peace with God through our Lord Jesus Christ" would not find the same traction in human affairs, and certainly not two millennia later (Romans 5:1).

What would it take for Christianity to find that traction again? I'm not talking about turning back the clock, which would be neither possible nor advisable. What might it look like for Christianity to function as a religion of grace today? Prescriptions may be a fool's errand, but predictions are another matter.

---

45. A trade-off of course, since payment is sometimes the only thing that gets us to show up and take it seriously.

First, for Christianity to be experienced as a religion of grace rather than law, it would speak about death more often than it currently does. That is, Christians would be just as willing to talk about the hereafter as they are about the here-and-now. Faith as a means to personal *or* social improvement would take a backseat to the more transcendent and eternal elements of Religion—of which there are many. Such a Christianity wouldn't simply talk *about* God but *to* God. Because ears habituated to the deafening rhythm of seculosity and the weary tune of "never enough" don't need fresh sheets of music. They crave the melody of absolution itself—a song that's emotional but not sentimental, personal but not individual, and never bashful about the liberating wind of Holy Spirit.

Second, a viable Christian faith would follow Christ's lead by focusing its attention on human motivation rather than behavior. Which means it would remember its own counsel that each of us—whether we're in the pews or not—is in bondage to forces outside of our control, whether they be inherited or assumed or some combination thereof. "A man can do what he wills, but he cannot will what he wills" is how philosopher Arthur Schopenhauer reportedly put it, paraphrasing the Pauline understanding that "what the heart desires, the will chooses, and the mind justifies." None of us are free agents making healthy decisions, and any message that addresses us as such will prove no more than a clanging cymbal.

Furthermore, the not-enoughness that haunts us is not an entirely false construct; we are not crazy for feeling, on some fundamental level, that we are in fact sinners. Everyone you meet is in some kind of pain, a swimmer caught in a riptide, sometimes of their own making.

Third, a grace-centered Christianity would be fundamentally Christ-centered. Sounds like a no-brainer, but what I mean is that it won't be consumer- or church-centered. As one of my favorite theologians is fond of saying, you can tell that the church has nothing of substance left to say when it starts talking primarily about itself. Instead, a religion of capital-G Grace would hold to Jesus Christ as the central revelation of who God is, and the cross as the central revelation of who Christ is—not just in terms of sacrificial love, but in terms of law-fulfilling righteousness imputed to nontransformed sinners like you and me. For this reason, a grace-centered Christianity would not balk from heralding—at full volume and without fingers crossed—the good news that *nothing that needs to be done hasn't already been done*. It would emphasize the counterintuitive announcement that enoughness is a gift, given freely to those who insist on paying, and at great cost to the giver. The only scorekeeping that matters has come to an end, regardless of how we might feel at the moment.

Then again, I wouldn't trust any roadmap drawn by someone caught in a riptide, regardless of how coherent or convincing a narrative he spins. Because our chief problem is not one of direction, or even the ocean itself. The chief problem is that we don't actually know how to swim.

What I mean is that the ultimate trouble with seculosity has nothing to do with soulmates or smartphones or tribalism or workaholism or even our compulsive desire to measure up. The common denominator is the human heart, yours and mine. Which is to say, the problem is sin. Sin is not something you can be talked out of ("stop controlling everything!") or coached through with the right wisdom. It is something from which you need to be saved—even when the nature of sin is that it lashes out at that which would rescue it.

And that's where all our narratives and religions break down for good, even ones of grace. Because no concept or framework, no matter how beautiful or beneficial, is going to breathe new life into limbs sunk to the bottom of the ocean. A God who saves those hellbent on stiff-arming his love is all that will do.

I only told my son half the story of The Day Your Grandfather Got Caught in a Riptide and Almost Died. The rest is too strange and too miraculous. You see, son, your grandfather relaxed into the current, but that only kept him alive long enough to be dragged out into the Atlantic. Yet it was there, in the overwhelming expanse of sea, bereft of hope, that your grandfather ran into him.

Some man in flippers was swimming past, likely training for a triathlon or some such thing. This angel of a deep-water enthusiast swooped in, hauled your grandfather to shore and then revived him. *That's* why he is alive today. He was rescued.

The End.

ACKNOWLEDGMENTS

Heartfelt thanks to Alex Field and everyone at The Bindery for getting the ball rolling and seeing it through. To my fantastic editor Tony Jones for taking a chance and shepherding this project with such care and tenacity (and to the illustrious Scott Jones for connecting us initially). To Paul Walker and my family at Christ Church Charlottesville for the one-in-a-million community of grace from which I draw so much. We are spoiled. To Aaron Zimmerman and the rest of the Mockingboard for their endless support and wisdom. To my cohosts on *The Mockingcast*, Sarah Condon and R. J. Heijmen, for helping me think through a lot of this material and making me laugh in the process. To David Peterson for compiling the early version of the text when he had much better things to do. To Kendall Gunther for hunting down citations and tying up loose ends—you are a lifesaver. To Ethan Richardson, C. J. Green, Margaret Pope, Bryan Jarrell, Luke Roland, and all my compatriots at Mockingbird for picking up the slack while my attention was divided and for being such terrific colleagues. To my in-laws, Ann and Tom West, for their overwhelming kindness, provision, and patience (and for covering with the boys when I had to be in the library!). To my brother JAZ for all the late-night calls, last-minute sermon advice, and disco treasures. To my parents, Mary and Paul Zahl, for the solid-rock foundation they still provide me and so many others. Your faithfulness, insight, and love astound me more with each passing year.

Extra enormous thanks go to my brother (and favorite theologian) Simeon Zahl for reading this manuscript and giving precious feedback at a time when his plate could not have been more full. I admire you so much. And to Will McDavid for his invaluable help and input every step of the way. Words really can't do my gratitude justice—and even if they could, you'd be the first person I'd run them by. Over pastrami if at all possible.

Finally, from the bottom of my heart, to CWZ, for her ceaseless sacrifice and encouragement. You were right about 60th Street and so much more. Love you to the barricade and beyond.

ENDNOTES

Intro

"A majority of Icelanders . . ." Rodney Stark, *The Triumph of Faith* (Wilmington, DE: ISI Books, 2015), 6, 45, 48.

"According to AppStore downloads . . ." Julie Beck, "The New Age of Astrology," *The Atlantic*, January 16, 2018, https://tinyurl .com/y7nv9o9x.

"He calls it 'a controlling story' . . ." David Dark, *Life's Too Short to Pretend You're Not Religious* (Downers Grove, IL: IVP Books, 2016), 14.

"Or 'the question of how . . .'" David Dark, *Life's Too Short to Pretend You're Not Religious* (Downers Grove, IL: IVP Books, 2016), 18.

"People are suffering and dying . . ." Will Storr, *Selfie: How We Became So Self-Obsessed and What It's Doing to Us* (London: Picador, 2017), 17.

"An obsession with righteousness . . ." Jonathan Haidt, *The Righteous Mind: Why Good People Are Divided by Politics and Religion* (New York: Vintage Books, 2013), xix–xx.

"There is no deeper pathos . . ." Reinhold Niebuhr, *An Interpretation of Christian Ethics* (Louisville: Westminster John Knox, 2013), 225.

"Philosopher Charles Taylor calls this . . ." Charles Taylor, *A Secular Age* (Cambridge, MA: Belknap, 2007), 299.

"Take me to your *secular* world.'" *Arrested Development*, season 2, episode 16, "Meat the Veals," directed by Joe Russo and written by Richard Rosenstock and Barbie Adler, aired April 3, 2005, on Fox.

Chapter 1 – Busyness

"She traveled to North Dakota . . ." Ethan Richardson, "The Overwhelm: A Conversation on a Modern Mandate with Brigid Schulte," *Mockingbird*, April 2, 2015, https://tinyurl.com/ybcsmocu.

"I'm not sure whether writing . . ." Brigid Schulte, *Overwhelmed: Work, Love, and Play When No One Has the Time* (New York: Farrar, Straus & Giroux, 2014), 45.

". . . keeping up with the Joneses . . ." Elizabeth Kolbert, "No Time," *The New Yorker*, May 26, 2014, https://tinyurl.com/ya62m5xu.

"Billy Mitchell makes for an entertaining . . ." Seth Gordon, dir., *The King of Kong: A Fistful of Quarters*, 2007, produced in association with LargeLab.

"To wit, the rash of 'suicide clusters' . . ." Hanna Rosin, "The Silicon Valley Suicides," *The Atlantic*, December 2015, https://tinyurl.com/ya84jgh5.

[footnote] "According to the cover story . . ." Hanna Rosin, "The Silicon Valley Suicides," *The Atlantic*, December 2015, https://tinyurl.com/ya84jgh5.

"The University of Pennsylvania made . . ." Julie Scelfo, "Suicide on Campus and the Pressure of Perfection," *New York Times*, July 27, 2015, https://tinyurl.com/yc4cs2od.

"Penn Face, the authors surmised, . . ." University of Pennsylvania, "Report of the Task Force on Student Psychological Health and Welfare," *Almanac Supplement*, February 17, 2015, https://tinyurl.com/yc2loky7.

[footnote] "The percentage of adults . . ." Monica Anderson and Andrew Perrin, "Technology Use among Seniors," *Pew Research Center*, May 17, 2017, https://tinyurl.com/n2euh9x.

[same footnote] "On the opposite end . . ." Brett Molina, "Read This Before You Give Your Kid His or Her First Smartphone," *USA Today*, December 10, 2017, https://tinyurl.com/yd2t93yz.

"A study published in 2018 . . ." Amandeep Dhir, Yossiri Yossatorn, Puneet Kaur, and Sufen Chen, "Online Social Media Fatigue and Psychological Wellbeing: A Study of Compulsive Use, Fear of Missing Out, Fatigue, Anxiety and Depression," *International Journal of Information Management* 40 (2018): 141–52.

"16-year-old Essena . . ." Stephanie McNeal, "An 18-Year-Old Instagram Star Says Her 'Perfect Life' Was Actually Making Her Miserable," *BuzzFeed*, November 4, 2015, https://tinyurl.com/yc8tf2oh.

"In her memoir *Cherry*, . . ." Mary Karr, *Cherry: A Memoir* (New York: Penguin, 2001), 101–17.

Chapter 2 – Romance

"Back in 1973, in his . . ." Ernest Becker, *The Denial of Death* (New York: Free Press, 1973), 159.

"Literary critic Stanley Fish . . ." Stanley Fish, "My Life Report," *New York Times*, October 31, 2011, https://tinyurl.com/y77jhf46.

"The vast majority of couples . . ." Carol Tavris and Elliot Aronson, *Mistakes Were Made (But Not by Me): Why We Justify Foolish Beliefs, Bad Decisions, and Hurtful Acts* (Boston: Mariner, 2015), 209, 217.

"One of the cruel betrayals . . ." Mark Greif, *Against Everything: Essays* (New York: Pantheon, 2016), 26.

"Exhibit A would have to be . . ." Helen Andrews, "Sex in the Meritocracy," *First Things*, January 19, 2013, https://tinyurl.com/ybg9dyfa.

"Many of us here have never . . ." Will Horowitz and Aliyya Swaby, "Elis Say Going Steady Can Be Rocky," *Yale Daily News*, February 12, 2010, https://tinyurl.com/yc6avoz6.

"For years, I turned distracted dudes . . ." Heather Havrilesky, "Ask Polly: Will My Semi-Available Boyfriend Ever Change?" *The Cut*, November 14, 2014, https://tinyurl.com/yaxandb8.

"For most of human history, . . ." Alain de Botton, *Why You Will Marry the Wrong Person* (London: The School of Life, 2017), 22–23.

"We come to one person, . . ." Esther Perel, "The Secret to Desire in a Long-Term Relationship," *TED*, February 2013, https://tinyurl.com/nd29njx.

"If your partner is your 'All' . . ." Ernest Becker, *The Denial of Death* (New York: Free Press, 1973), 167.

"[The internet] doesn't simply help . . ." Aziz Ansari, *Modern Romance* (New York: Penguin, 2016), 125.

"We don't divorce—or have affairs . . ." Esther Perel, "Rethinking Infidelity: A Talk for Anyone Who Has Ever Loved," *TED*, March 2015, https://tinyurl.com/y8lbr4fl.

"Perhaps it looks a bit . . ." Molly Howes, "The Radiance, Then the Ashes," *New York Times*, June 9, 2011, https://tinyurl.com/y8adks3p.

"Compatibility is an achievement . . ." Alain de Botton, *Why You Will Marry the Wrong Person* (London: The School of Life, 2017), 51.

"I was human with this person, . . ." Paul F. M. Zahl, *Grace in Practice: A Theology of Everyday Life* (Grand Rapids: Eerdmans, 2007), 139–40.

Chapter 3 – Parenting

". . . to assuage our anxiety . . ." indebted to Oliver Burkeman, "The Diabolical Genius of the Baby Advice Industry," *The Guardian*, January 16, 2018, https://tinyurl.com/yaq7mdn2.

"A recent study has shown that if . . ." Sarah Miller, "New Parenting Study Released," *The New Yorker*, March 24, 2014, https://tinyurl.com/y9d77rft.

"A recent cartoon spells out . . ." Robert Leighton, "A Father Leans In to Give Advice to His Son," *The New Yorker*, February 11, 2013.

"Adam Strassberg, a psychiatrist . . ." Adam Strassberg, "Guest Opinion: Keep Calm and Parent On," *Palo Alto Online*, Mar 16, 2015, https://tinyurl.com/y8wtbmra.

"A high-school teacher in a suburb . . ." Frank Bruni, "Best, Brightest—and Saddest?" *New York Times*, April 11, 2015, https://tinyurl.com/yb5xsoep.

"When parents have tended to do . . ." Julie Lythcott-Haims, *How to Raise an Adult: Break Free of the Overparenting Trap and Prepare Your Kid for Success* (New York: Henry Holt, 2015), 90–91.

"A lot of parents today . . ." Amy Chua, "Tiger Mom's Long-Distance Cub," *Wall Street Journal*, December 24, 2011, https://tinyurl.com/yabrqc8d.

"One image that has helped me . . ." paraphrased in part from David Zahl, *A Mess of Help: From the Crucified Soul of Rock 'N' Roll* (Charlottesville, VA: Mockingbird Ministries, 2014), 116–17.

"I've always maintained—and I still do . . ." Jeff Baenen, "Westerberg Straddles Musical Styles," *Deseret News*, October 1, 2004, https://tinyurl.com/y73fse8w.

"Questions about vegetable intake, . . ." Sarah Condon, "On Blessed Messes and the New Law of Mothering Ineptitude," *Mockingbird*, March 29, 2014, https://tinyurl.com/y9oeg6br.

"All of those things I never imagined . . ." Carrie Willard, "The Mother I Was Going to Be," *Mockingbird*, January 27, 2017, https://tinyurl.com/ya54a7ta.

"I can't help but wonder . . ." Katie Roiphe, "Modern Parenting," *Slate*, November 21, 2010, https://tinyurl.com/ycq23lwb.

"Ronan Rapp was born . . ." Emily Rapp, "Notes from a Dragon Mom," *New York Times*, October 15, 2011, https://tinyurl.com/y9bv2dsd. See also Emily Rapp, *The Still Point of the Turning World* (New York: Penguin, 2013), 19–21.

"A 'noncontingent, compassionate alliance' . . ." Dorothy W. Martyn, *Beyond Deserving: Children, Parents, and Responsibility Revisited* (Grand Rapids: Eerdmans, 2007), xv.

"The law says 'do this,' . . ." Martin Luther, *Luther's Works: Career of the Reformer*, ed. Harold J. Grimm and Helmut T.

Lehmann (St. Louis: Concordia Publishing House; Minneapolis: Fortress Press, 1957), 41.

Chapter 4 – Technology

"When the bell rings, you get up . . ." Jean Renoir, *Renoir, My Father*, trans. Randolph Weaver and Dorothy Weaver (New York: New York Review of Books, 2001), 245.

"The Internet launders outrage . . ." James Hamblin, "My Outrage Is Better Than Your Outrage," *The Atlantic*, July 31, 2015, https://tinyurl.com/y7bg28fg.

[footnote] "In a relevant article on the . . ." R. Scott Clark, "Is Efficiency a Virtue in the Church?" *The Heidelblog*, January 5, 2015, https://tinyurl.com/y7vr5g5g.

"Technosolutionism explains why Mark Zuckerberg . . ." Farhad Manjoo, "Can Facebook Fix Its Own Worst Bug?" *New York Times Magazine*, April 25, 2017, https://tinyurl.com/mdk7vp9.

". . . idea of humanity attempting to overcome . . ." Meghan O'Gieblyn, "Ghost in the Cloud," *n+1* 28 (Spring 2017): https://tinyurl.com/lsy8sx9.

". . . tend to sound an awful lot . . ." Meghan O'Gieblyn, "Ghost in the Cloud," *n+1* 28 (Spring 2017): https://tinyurl.com/lsy8sx9.

"Believe it or not, the word transhuman . . ." *Oxford English Dictionary Online*, s.v. "transhuman, adj.," OED Online, http://www.oed.com/Entry/204784?redirectedFrom=transhuman.

"Back in 2013 some brave individual . . ." Åse Dragland, "Big Data—For Better or Worse," *Sintef*, May 22, 2013, https://tinyurl.com/yd7m3dpo.

"The *Wall Street Journal* reported on a friendly . . ." Rachel Bachman, "Want to Cheat Your Fitbit? Try a Puppy or a Power Drill," *Wall Street Journal*, June 19, 2016, https://tinyurl.com /yb4uv3k8.

"Journalist Elizabeth Minkel hinted at . . ." Elizabeth Minkel, "ICYMI: The Internet Has Ruined Our Conception of Time," *New Statesman*, May 23, 2014, https://tinyurl.com/y8nadwj2.

"Historical parallels for this phenomenon . . ." Oliver Burkeman, "Why Time Management Is Ruining Our Lives," *The Guardian*, December 22, 2016, https://tinyurl.com/h5x4oc9.

"Maybe dullness is associated . . ." David Foster Wallace, *The Pale King* (New York: Little, Brown, 2011), 85.

". . . to push back 'against the indignity of being made to wait.'" Joshua Rothman, "A New Theory of Distraction," *The New Yorker*, June 16, 2015, https://tinyurl.com/y7rrkanp. See also Matthew Crawford, *The World beyond Your Head: On Becoming an Individual in an Age of Distraction* (New York: Farrar, Straus & Giroux, 2015).

"The reason we live in a culture . . ." Andrew Sullivan, "I Used to Be a Human Being," *New York Magazine*, September 19, 2016, https://tinyurl.com/ya6bl78o.

". . . the 'Mediator and Advocate' who suffered . . ." *The Book of Common Prayer, The Holy Eucharist Rite One, Prayers of the People* (New York: Church Publishing Incorporated, 1979), 330.

"In fact, several studies of online behavior . . ." Ashley Anderson, Dominique Brossard, Dietram A. Scheufele, Michael Z. Xenos, and Peter Ladwig, "The 'Nasty Effect:' Online Incivility and Risk Perceptions of Emerging Technologies," *The Journal of Computer-Mediated Communication* 19, no. 3 (April 2014): 373–87, https://doi.org/10.1111/jcc4.12009.

"Once we realize that we can . . ." Ted Peters, *Sin Boldly! Justifying Faith for Fragile and Broken Souls* (Minneapolis: Fortress Press, 2015), 39.

". . . a comma, not a period." Martin Luther King Jr., "Eulogy for Martyred Children, Sermon delivered on 9/18/63," in *Martin Luther King, Jr. Treasury* (Yonkers, NY: Educational Heritage, 1964), 139–40.

Chapter 5 – Work

"True story: in 1965, the US Senate . . ." Congressional Record, January 12, 1965, 619.

[footnote] "In 1930 pioneering economist John Maynard Keynes . . ." John Maynard Keynes, "Economic Possibilities for Our Grandchildren (1930)," in *Essays in Persuasion* (New York: Harcourt, Brace, 1932), 358–73.

"A cartoon strip that went viral . . ." Alex Gregory, "I Am Not a Workaholic. I Just Work to Relax," *The New Yorker*, August 27, 2007.

"*The Onion* memorably lampooned . . ." "Laid-Back Company Allows Employees to Work from Home after 6PM," *The Onion*, November 4, 2014, https://tinyurl.com/y9sx99mu.

"As one of Amazon's running office jokes . . ." David Streitfel and Christine Haughney, "Expecting the Unexpected from Jeff Bezos," *New York Times*, August 17, 2013, https://tinyurl.com/y9ncafgm.

"Everyone wants to be a model employee . . ." Dan Lyons, "In Silicon Valley, Working 9 to 5 Is for Losers," *New York Times*, August 31, 2017, https://tinyurl.com/ydef8nsa. See also Carolyn

Said, "Suicide of an Uber Engineer: Widow Blames Job Stress," *San Francisco Chronicle*, April 25, 2017, https://tinyurl.com/y7uf6voq.

"The eclipsing of life's other complications . . .'" Ryan Avent, "Why Do We Work So Hard?" *1843 Magazine*, April/May 2016, https://tinyurl.com/jgb6h9v.

"On average, employers granted new . . ." Daniel Engber, "Quit Whining about Your Sick Colleague," *New York Times*, December 29, 2014, https://tinyurl.com/y6u6g8jm.

"In 2010, the American Psychological Association . . ." Audrey Hamilton, "Psychology of Procrastination: Why People Put Off Important Tasks Until the Last Minute," *American Psychological Association*, April 5, 2010, https://tinyurl.com/36dj8pu.

". . . a larger percentage than those . . ." Debra J. Brody, Laura A. Pratt, and Jeffery P. Hughes, "Prevalence of Depression Among Adults Aged 20 and Over: United States, 2013–2016," NCHS Data Brief no. 303, February 2018, Centers for Disease Control and Prevention, https://tinyurl.com/y987hgoq.

"A separate study a few years . . ." Timothy A. Pychyl, Jonathan M. Lee, Rachelle Thibodeau, and Allan Blunt, "Five Days of Emotion: An Experience Sampling Study of Undergraduate Student Procrastination," *Journal of Social Behavior and Personality* 15, no. 5 (2000): 239–54.

"Procrastination as epidemic . . ." Anna Della Subin, "How to Stop Time," *New York Times*, September 26, 2014, https://tinyurl.com/y9k4jzu7.

"The snow cares not for your deadlines . . ." David Dudley, "In Case of Blizzard, Do Nothing," *New York Times*, January 22, 2016, https://tinyurl.com/y7pyb7xk.

"If the world could have lived . . ." Robert Farrar Capon, *Kingdom, Grace, Judgment: Paradox, Outrage, and Vindication in the Parables of Jesus* (Grand Rapids: Eerdmans, 2002), 222.

"One trenchant example of what . . ." Erin Callan, "Is There Life after Work?" *New York Times*, March 9, 2013, https://tinyurl.com/y7yzsvrr.

Chapter 6 – Leisure

"SoulCycle may be the most popular . . ." Tara Isabella Burton, "CrossFit Is My Church," *Vox*, September 10, 2018, https://tinyurl.com/y8ou2kda.

"Alongside the spiritualization . . ." indebted to Heather Havrilesky, *What If This Were Enough? Essays* (New York: Doubleday, 2018), 173–77.

"One of my favorite humor websites . . ." "New Nike Running App Tells You What You're Really Running From," *The Onion*, August 12, 2014, https://tinyurl.com/y857t9nq.

"Dr. Peter Gray, a psychologist at Boston . . ." Peter Gray, "Play as a Foundation for Hunter-Gatherer Social Existence," *American Journal of Play* 1, no. 4 (2009): 476–522.

"He goes on to report that . . ." Peter Gray, "The Decline of Play and the Rise of Psychopathology in Children and Adolescents," *American Journal of Play* 3, no. 4 (2011): 444.

"The cost of this relentless . . ." Madeline Levine, *Teach Your Children Well: Why Values and Coping Skills Matter More Than Grades, Trophies, or "Fat Envelopes"* (New York: Harper Perennial, 2012), 12.

"Books about 'playful parenting' . . ." Audie Cornish, "What Kids Can Learn from a Water Balloon Fight," *All Things Considered*, NPR, June 25, 2014.

"Play helps children . . . learn . . ." Peter Gray, "The Decline of Play and the Rise of Psychopathology in Children and Adolescents," *American Journal of Play* 3, no. 4 (2011): 454.

"I'm fairly certain that there . . ." Ellen Gamerman, "Competitive about Your Meditation? Relax, Everyone Else Is Too," *Wall Street Journal*, June 12, 2018, https://tinyurl.com/ydf7wdr8.

"Companies like insurance giant Aetna . . ." Joe Pinsker, "Corporations' Newest Productivity Hack: Meditation," *The Atlantic*, March 10, 2015, https://tinyurl.com/yc5ps28r. Emphasis added.

"In late 2014, the Center for . . ." "Insufficient Sleep Is a Public Health Epidemic," Centers for Disease Control and Prevention, January 13, 2014, http://www.cdc.gov/features/dssleep/ (page now defunct).

"Over the past decade or so, the sleep . . ." Eve Fairbanks, "How Did Sleep Become So Nightmarish?" March 21, 2014, *The New York Times Magazine*, https://tinyurl.com/yb8xcmca.

"Given our conflicted relationship . . ." Walter Brueggemann, *Sabbath as Resistance: Saying No to the Culture of Now* (Louisville: Westminster John Knox, 2014), xiv.

"The alternative on offer . . ." Walter Brueggemann, *Sabbath as Resistance: Saying No to the Culture of Now* (Louisville: Westminster John Knox, 2014), xiv.

"It is impossible to gain peace . . ." Martin Luther, *A Commentary on St. Paul's Epistle to the Galatians*, trans. Theodore Graebner, Modern History Sourcebook, Fordham University, https://tinyurl.com/yaoe9mza.

Chapter 7 – Food

"Uh, I'm only here for the ninety-nine-cent . . ." Jay Karas, dir., *Jim Gaffigan: Mr. Universe* (Burbank, CA: New Wave Entertainment, 2012).

"Food now expresses the symbolic values . . ." William Deresiewicz, "A Matter of Taste?" *New York Times*, October 26, 2012, https://tinyurl.com/ydhmnjuf.

"Every single choice we make . . ." Alice Waters, "Alice Waters Applies a 'Delicious Revolution' to School Food," *Center for Ecoliteracy*, June 29, 2009, https://tinyurl.com/y9935ecn.

"Orthorexia starts out as an innocent attempt . . ." Karin Kratina, comp., "Orthorexia Nervosa," *National Eating Disorders Association*, 2012, https://tinyurl.com/yauwsgtq.

"I become what journalist Joyce Wadler . . ." Joyce Wadler, "The Dieting Supremacist. Hate Her," *New York Times*, April 4, 2014, https://tinyurl.com/y73qbag2.

"The way that we are taught to think . . ." "Tell Me I'm Fat," *This American Life*, June 17, 2016, https://tinyurl.com/y8x42rao.

"Robert Capon once wrote . . ." Robert Farrar Capon, *Health, Money, and Love—And Why We Don't Enjoy Them* (Grand Rapids: Eerdmans, 1990), 161.

Chapter 8 – Politics

"I'm. In. Loooooove." *Seinfeld*, season 6, episode 5, "The Couch," directed by Andy Ackerman and written by Larry David, aired October 27, 1994, on NBC.

"In the late 1950s, when American . . ." Lynn Vavrek, "A Measure of Identity: Are You Wedded to Your Party?," *New York Times*, January 31, 2017, https://tinyurl.com/y7s7rf4j.

[footnote] "By way of contrast, when respondents . . ." Frank Newport, "In U.S., 87% Approve of Black-White Marriage, vs. 4% in 1958," *Gallup*, July 25, 2013, https://tinyurl.com/yboqa4sc.

"This makes sense when you . . ." "Political Polarization in the American Public," *Pew Research Center*, June 12, 2014, https://tinyurl.com/p4scahz.

"As if we needed more proof . . ." Michele Margolis, *From Politics to the Pews: How Partisanship and the Political Environment Shape Religious Identity* (Chicago: University of Chicago Press, 2018).

"In his aptly titled book *The Righteous Mind* . . ." Jonathan Haidt, *The Righteous Mind: Why Good People Are Divided by Politics and Religion* (New York: Vintage Books, 2013), 122–54, 169–76.

"As *The Onion* once joked . . ." "'We Can Have Differences of Opinion and Still Respect Each Other,' Says Betrayer of the One True Cause," May 1, 2018, *The Onion*, https://tinyurl.com/y8wv4yad.

"The business of correcting idealism . . ." Stephen Marche, *The Unmade Bed: The Messy Truth about Men and Women in the 21st Century* (New York: Simon & Schuster, 2017), 159.

"Many people are drawn to defend . . ." James Hamblin, "My Outrage Is Better Than Your Outrage," *The Atlantic*, July 31, 2015, https://tinyurl.com/y7bg28fg.

"Harambe perhaps?" Madison Park and Holly Yan, "Gorilla Killing: 3-Year-Old Boy's Mother Won't Be Charged," *CNN*, June 6, 2016, https://tinyurl.com/y8wpqfgp.

"Essayist Jon Baskin put his finger . . ." Jon Baskin, "Tired of Winning," *The Point*, Spring 2018, https://tinyurl.com/ybpb76pm.

"The feminist writer and activist . . ." Vivian Gornick, "What Independence Has Come to Mean to Me: The Pain of Solitude, the Pleasures of Self-Knowledge," in *The Bitch in the House: 26*

Women Tell the Truth about Sex, Solitude, Work, Motherhood, and Marriage, ed. Cathi Hanauer (New York: William Morrow, 2002), 259.

"That the dream of a Perfect . . ." W. H. Auden, "For the Time Being: A Christmas Oratorio," in *Collected Poems*, ed. Edward Mendelson (New York: Modern Library, 2007), 374.

"Fast forward a couple years, and . . ." Seth Stephens-Davidowitz, "Everybody Lies: How Google Search Reveals Our Darkest Secrets," *The Guardian*, July 9, 2017, https://tinyurl.com/ybuo46mu.

Chapter 9 – Jesusland

"The word *law* is a broad one . . ." For a longer discussion of the relation of law and grace, see William McDavid, Ethan Richardson, and David Zahl, *Law and Gospel: A Theology for Sinners and Saints* (Charlottesville, VA: Mockingbird Ministries, 2015).

"The pillars, but . . . also the dynamite . . ." Aldous Huxley, *Time Must Have a Stop* (Normal, IL: Dalkey Archive Press, 2001), 234.

"What he meant was the same thing . . ." William Faulkner, "Banquet Speech," The Nobel Prize, December 10, 1950, https://tinyurl.com/y7voh25l.

"I do not understand my own actions . . ." Hannah Arendt, "The Apostle Paul and the Impotence of the Will" in *The Life of the Mind*, 2 vols. (New York: Harcourt, Brace, 1978), 2:63–73.

"Just ask Markus Persson . . ." Julie Bort, "'I've Never Felt More Isolated': The Man Who Sold Minecraft to Microsoft for $2.5 Billion Reveals the Empty Side of Success," *The Independent*, September 29, 3016, https://tinyurl.com/ybpyedud.

"Entrepreneurial dynamo Elon Musk . . ." Neil Strauss, "Elon Musk: The Architect of Tomorrow," *Rolling Stone*, November 15, 2017, https://tinyurl.com/yaeeshl3.

"Lady Gaga as well." Maria Cavassuto, "Lady Gaga: Fame Is the Most Isolating Thing in the World," *Variety*, June 3, 2016, https://tinyurl.com/yatdztjl.

". . . he hints at the possibility . . ." C. S. Lewis, *The Lion, the Witch and the Wardrobe* (New York: HarperTrophy, 2002), 171.

"Grace moves beyond deserving . . ." Dorothy W. Martyn, *Beyond Deserving: Children, Parents, and Responsibility Revisited* (Grand Rapids: Eerdmans, 2007), 63.

"Pretty soon you're living in a spiritualized . . ." Bob Mankoff, "I Can't Promise I'll Change, but I Can Promise I'll *Pretend* to Change," *The New Yorker*, August 2, 1999.

". . . the One 'whose property is always to have mercy.'" *The Book of Common Prayer, The Holy Eucharist Rite One, Prayer of Humble Access* (New York: Church Publishing Incorporated, 1979), 337.

[footnote] ". . . the league of the guilty." Francis Spufford, *Unapologetic: Why, Despite Everything, Christianity Can Still Make Surprising Emotional Sense* (San Francisco: HarperOne, 2013), 48.

"When I was a Christian . . ." Frances Lee, "Excommunicate Me from the Church of Social Justice," *Autostraddle*, July 13, 2017, https://tinyurl.com/y7ezarul.

"To borrow a fancy phrase . . ." Charles Taylor, *A Secular Age* (Cambridge, MA: Belknap, 2007), 539.

"That is to say, Christianity at its . . ." William McDavid, Ethan Richardson, and David Zahl, *Law and Gospel: A Theology for Sinners and Saints* (Charlottesville, VA: Mockingbird Ministries, 2015), 21.

"Imagine walking into a church . . ." John Z. and Tom B., *Grace in Addiction* (Charlottesville, VA: Mockingbird Ministries, 2010), 7.

"Technically Christians need their own . . ." Helen Andrews, "AA Envy," *The Hedgehog Review* 17, no. 3 (Fall 2015): https://tinyurl.com/yaogko58.

"In 1958, the great American poet . . ." Langston Hughes, "Thank you, M'am," in *Short Stories*, ed. Akiba Sullivan Harper (New York: Hill & Wang, 1996), 226.

Conclusion – What to "Do" about It

"They account for about a hundred deaths . . ." Maggie Astor, "How to Survive a Rip Current: First, Don't Fight It," *New York Times*, July 31, 2017, https://tinyurl.com/ya2oju64.

". . . the strange persistence of guilt . . ." Wilfred M. McClay, "The Strange Persistence of Guilt," *The Hedgehog Review* 19, no. 1 (Spring 2017): https://tinyurl.com/yb4k3gmv.

"'How is such a belief . . .'" Walker Percy, "Questions They Never Asked Me," in *Conversations with Walker Percy*, ed. Lewis A. Lawson and Victor A. Kramer (Jackson: University Press of Mississippi, 1985), 175.

"What the heart desires, the will chooses . . ." Ashley Null, "Dr. Ashley Null on Thomas Cranmer," *Anglican Church League*, September 2001, https://tinyurl.com/y7qb7o8o.

"As one of my favorite theologians . . ." Steven Paulson, "The Augustinian Imperfection," in *The Gospel of Justification in Christ: Where Does the Church Stand Today?*, ed. Wayne C. Stumme (Grand Rapids: Eerdmans, 2006), 104–24.